FIFTY SIGNS

OF THE

End Times

Are We Living in the Last Days?

DAVID SCOTT NICHOLS, MD

CROSSBOOKS
PUBLISHING

CrossBooks™
A Division of LifeWay
1663 Liberty Drive
Bloomington, IN 47403
www.crossbooks.com
Phone: 1-866-879-0502

Unless otherwise noted, all Scripture verses are taken from the Holy
Bible, New International Version, Copyright 1973, 1978, 1984
Biblica. Used by permission of Zondervan. All rights reserved.
Emphasis Added by author

Scripture quotations marked NKJV are from the
New King James Version of the Bible.

First published by CrossBooks 09/17/2012

ISBN: 978-1-4627-2059-0 (sc)
ISBN: 978-1-4627-2061-3 (hc)
ISBN: 978-1-4627-2060-6 (e)

Library of Congress Control Number: 2012914576

Printed in the United States of America

To Sandy,
My Wife, My Love

TABLE OF CONTENTS

TABLE OF FIGURES

ACKNOWLEDGMENT

I WANT TO thank several very special people who have helped in the writing of this book. First of all, I would like to thank my parents for raising me in a Christian home and showing me the true meaning of love, honor, and commitment. Because of them, I was led to Christ at an early age. Although they went to be with Jesus when I was still very young, they had already instilled in me important biblical principles that have been invaluable throughout my lifetime. My mother was the epitome of selfless love. My father was a man of great courage and honor.

Although I have been teaching and writing on the Bible for many years, it was really due to the loving encouragement of my beautiful wife, Sandy, that I decided to write *Fifty Signs of the End Times* for publication. Neither of us understood the many hours of work that would be required to bring this book to publication. She has truly been a tremendous help throughout the entire process.

God blessed Sandy and me with two great children, Laura and Christine. Although they each have extremely busy schedules, they were happy to help their father in the editing process. Their input was very helpful and much appreciated.

Finally, I want to acknowledge my sister, Margaret Nichols, and her husband, Dan Van Duyne. They both spent many hours of time carefully editing the book. Their suggestions were excellent. In fact, it really is amazing how much effort and time all of these great family members contributed to the process of writing this book.

Before beginning the book, I would like to make one additional acknowledgement. Dr. Grant Jeffrey, a great man, writer, teacher, and prophecy scholar, has just recently gone on to be with the Lord. I met Dr. Jeffrey at a prophecy conference several years ago and spoke with him about some of my future plans in regard to teaching and writing. He took the time to answer my questions and offer encouragement. He showed himself to be a very kind and caring gentleman.

His untimely passing occurred just a few weeks prior to this book being sent to the publisher. Grant has often acknowledged his loving and special relationship with his wife, Kaye. My prayers are with her and the rest of his family and friends.

Dr. Jeffrey was an extremely respected prophecy writer and teacher for the past twenty-five years. He also hosted a popular television show. He was a prolific writer on the topic of end-times prophecy. All of his books are excellent and reveal his outstanding knowledge and expertise in the field of eschatology. The reader will note several quotes from Dr. Jeffrey's books while reading *Fifty Signs of the End Times*. The world lost a very important Christian scholar when Grant Jeffrey went to be with the Lord.

PREFACE

A S MOST READERS of this book would agree, there has been no scarcity of "end-of-the-world" predictions in recent decades. Obviously, so far, none have come true. However, that does not stop new predictions from regularly coming forth. Even now, there is significant hype attached to the date, December 21, 2012. That is when many believe the world as we know it will cease to exist. Frankly, the many authors who are now writing on this topic disagree on exactly what will occur on that day. Some say that there will be a series of widespread catastrophic events due to the magnetic poles of the earth reversing their polarity. Others suggest that there will be some esoteric resetting of the balance of nature; still others have their own unique theories concerning the fate of the earth on that particular date. As it turns out, this day has been chosen, almost exclusively, due to the fact that the ancient Mayan calendar concludes with that date in history. In other words, there is little evidence to suggest that these "prophets of doom" will be correct.

Over the past several decades, there have been many other predictions and theories relating to the day the world will end. Some people have even claimed a biblical basis for their prediction. The problem with that, however, is that the Bible says no one will know the day or the hour of the return of the Messiah. "No one knows about that day or hour, not even the angels in heaven, nor the Son, but only the Father" (Matt 24:36). That quote from Jesus is quite clear. No one knows when Jesus will return... no one, but God, Himself.

So, that being the case, why have I written this book? The fact is that the Bible does say that, although no one can know the exact date of the Second Coming of Jesus Christ, those who watch for the signs of the times can know when the *season* of His return has arrived. In His sermon concerning the end times, Jesus taught on this topic, "Now learn this lesson from the fig tree: as soon as its twigs get tender and its leaves come out, you know that summer is near. Even so, when you see all these things, you know that it is near, right at the door" (Matt 24:32-33). That time has come.

Ever since I was a teenager, I have been fascinated by end-times prophecy. Although early on, I read books other than the Bible to see what they had to say on this topic, it did not take long for me to realize that none of these other "prophets" gave any evidence to support their claims. In fact, their predictions were either too vague to be of any value or else they were eventually proven to be incorrect. The writings of people such as Edgar Cayce, Jeanne Dixon, and Nostradamus have often been consulted by people wondering what the future will bring. There is absolutely no logical reason for anyone to believe the predictions of these non-biblical prophets. They have done nothing to demonstrate that they have the supernatural power to predict the future accurately. However, God has given mankind excellent reasons to believe that His Word, the Holy Bible, does foretell the future.

The Bible is the only book in the world that challenges its readers to prove (or refute) that it is truly God's Word. No other holy book does this because that challenge cannot be met by any other religion. God gives significant evidence to demonstrate that the Bible is truly His Word through His use of hundreds of prophecies in both the Old and New Testaments. Incredibly, a full one-quarter of the Bible is prophecy. Hundreds of Bible prophecies have already been fulfilled;

God has made no mistakes. Twenty-five hundred years ago, God said "I am God, and there is no other; I am God, and there is none like me. I make known the end from the beginning, from ancient times, what is still to come. I say: My purpose will stand, and I will do all that I please." (Isaiah 46:9-10). Jesus taught, "I have told you now before it happens, so that when it does happen, you will believe." (John 14:29). A great many books have been written to demonstrate the accuracy of biblical prophecies. For example, Barton Payne has written an *Encyclopedia of Biblical Prophecy* detailing well over one thousand of these amazing predictions. The vast majority are very specific. Even specific names, dates, and places where certain events are to take place are prophesied all throughout the Bible, long before these events occurred. No God would create a challenge of this magnitude, which would be so easy to refute, unless He was absolutely sure that He would pass the test. Indeed, God and His Bible have passed this test.

There are many additional reasons for people to trust the Bible. In contrast to all other religions, dozens of excellent books on the subject of Christian apologetics have been written. For readers who have any doubts concerning the absolute truth of the Bible, I suggest that they carefully read one or more of the books listed in Appendix 3. Outstanding reasons to believe will be found in all of those books and should convince virtually any person that the Bible is the actual inerrant Word of God. Of course, this assumes that they will be read with an open, prayerful, and searching mind. Armed with this confidence, Christians can study the prophecies concerning the end times and actually know when world events begin to signal that the end of this age is near. God did give us many signs to look for during this time in history, and He wants us to be aware of them.

Several hundred hours have gone into the study of all of the end-time signs presented in this book. The Bible has been thoroughly researched to locate and report on every sign God prophesied would be present just prior to His Son's return. Armed with these prophecies, a comprehensive review of all available information, written and audio-visual (using movies, television, and the Internet), was undertaken by this author to find out whether these prophecies have been fulfilled. This book is also completely up to date with current world events. Incredibly, virtually all of the prophecies that the Bible says will take place in the latter days have recently come to fruition. With only a couple of exceptions, as will be seen, these prophecies have been fulfilled within the last sixty years. Most have actually taken place within the past twenty years.

Although there are many fine books currently on the market on the topic of the end times, there are none that I have seen that include the comprehensive treatment and analysis found in this book. My goal is to present a complete listing of these biblical signs in one easily referenced and understandable source, while also providing an interesting, yet reasonably succinct, explanation of each of these fulfilled prophecies. Each sign discussed in this book is coupled with its appropriate Bible prophecy to demonstrate just how each has been fulfilled. I do not believe that there are any significant end-time prophecies that have been omitted. In fact, I managed to mention a few more than the fifty noted in the title.

It is my sincere belief that the omnipotent God of the universe has communicated with His creation through the Holy Bible. As will become evident in the pages that follow, we have entered into the time in history that will likely soon result in the Second Coming of the Messiah, Jesus. I hope that the reading of this book will encourage Christians to always remember that God has everything under His perfect control as we approach the coming Rapture. I also pray that it will convince many skeptics to engage in any and all necessary biblical study required in order to come to a clear understanding of the powerful truth of God's Word. As the writer of the Book of Hebrews noted, God is a "rewarder of those who diligently seek Him" (Heb 11:6). I am confident that He will lead them to an understanding of the Truth.

Introduction -
Are We Living in the Last Days?

S INCE HAL LINDSEY'S *Late Great Planet Earth* book hit bookshelves in the early 1970s, public fascination with the topic of end-times prophecy has increased. Several other authors have come out with similarly popular books since that time. Unfortunately, as previously mentioned, there have been some who have set actual dates as to when the Rapture and/or the Second Coming would occur. For example, 1988 was a year that many date-setters claimed was to be the year of the Rapture. This was primarily due to the fact that 1988 was the fortieth anniversary of Israel regaining their status as an independent nation. On October 20, 1991, a full-page advertisement was featured in USA Today claiming that Jesus would return sometime on October 28, 1992.

Many may remember that there were those who thought that the year A.D. 2000 would be the end of the world. Now, December 21, 2012 is currently the most popular date for those who like to set these apocalyptic dates. However, plenty of others have been suggested. Harold Camping, a well-known preacher from California, recently looked forward to judgment day; he was convinced that it would come on May 21, 2011... then later on, October 21, 2011. He was obviously wrong.

As was already noted in the preface, the Bible makes it very clear that no one on earth will know the exact date of the Second Coming of the Messiah. However, the followers of Christ are encouraged to watch expectantly for the signs that will herald His return. The Bible presents scores of signs that will be present in the world as the end times approach.

In order to understand how these signs relate to the coming events of the last days, it will be important to know the proposed order of these future events. Therefore, before getting to the main portion of this book, a brief explanation of the biblical view of the end times is in order. Without this information, it would be much more difficult to see how each sign relates to the coming of the Lord.

Eschatology is the term used to describe the study of the last days. Since the Bible is the Word of God, we can always trust what it says. Given the proven fact that hundreds of prophecies have already been fulfilled, one can come to the logical conclusion that all of the prophecies dealing with future events will also come true. However, it is important to note that there are different viewpoints that very committed Christian scholars take concerning these latter day events. For example, there is a difference of opinion on when the Rapture of the church will occur. There are also differing opinions on exactly what is meant by the Millennium and how it relates to the Second Coming of the Messiah. However, almost all prophecy scholars do agree that there will be a terrible time of tribulation (of seven years duration) just prior to this glorious event.

The viewpoint taken in this book has also become the most popular among prophecy teachers since Israel once again became an independent nation in 1948. Through the reading of this book, it will become evident that the nation and people of Israel are participants in more than half of the end-time prophetic signs. Frankly, given that the nation of Israel did not exist for almost two thousand years, it is understandable that it was difficult for many Bible scholars, prior to the mid-twentieth century, to believe that

Israel would have a significant role to play in the latter days. Now that it is once again a thriving nation, it is no longer very difficult to see how Israel will actually play a central part in the end times.

The technical terminology for the eschatological belief system espoused in this book can be stated in the following manner: there will be a *premillennial* return of Jesus preceded by a *pretribulation Rapture* of the church. Stated another way, Christ will return to earth to set up His Millennial Kingdom at the conclusion of a seven year period of *Tribulation*. The Rapture of the church will take place just before this Tribulation. In order to understand how some of the fifty signs of the end times presented in this book will lead to these latter day events, it will be of value to briefly review many of the coming events leading to the Second Coming of Jesus. Their likely order of occurrence is as follows:

- The Rapture of the church - "For the Lord himself will come down from heaven, with a loud command, with the voice of the archangel and with the trumpet call of God, and the dead in Christ will rise first. [17]After that, we who are still alive and are left will be caught up together with them in the clouds to meet the Lord in the air. And so we will be with the Lord forever" (1 Thess 4:16-17).
- Israel will be involved in war with their neighbors around the time of the Rapture. These battles likely will come just before and soon after the Rapture. At some point, Russia will also be an enemy combatant. God will protect Israel in all of these wars and they will always emerge victorious.
- During the time just after the Rapture of the church, a very charismatic man will emerge from the European Community and assume the position of world leader. He will be the infamous Antichrist.
- A seven year Tribulation will follow the signing of a treaty between Israel and several of their neighbors. This treaty will

3

be brokered by the Antichrist. The Tribulation will be a time of God's judgment on those nations and people who have rejected Him. "War will continue until the end, and desolations have been decreed.[27] He [the Antichrist] will confirm a covenant with many for one 'seven'" (Dan 9:26-27).

- A global government and one world apostate religion will dominate the first 3 ½ years of the Tribulation. God's judgment upon the world will begin to be felt in a very significant way.

- At the halfway point of this seven year period, the Antichrist will come into the rebuilt Jewish Temple, desecrate it, and claim to be God, Himself. With the help of his right-hand man, the False Prophet, He will demand to be worshipped and obeyed. "In the middle of the 'seven' he will put an end to sacrifice and offering. And on a wing [of the temple] he will set up an abomination that causes desolation, until the end that is decreed is poured out on him" (Dan 9:27).

- The judgment of God and the wrath of Satan will both be felt during the Great Tribulation, the last 3 ½ years of the seven year Tribulation. No period of destruction has ever been seen to equal this time in human history. "From the time that the daily sacrifice is abolished and the abomination that causes desolation is set up, there will be 1,290 days" (Dan 12:11).

- As the Tribulation draws to a close and just as Satan and the Antichrist are about to defeat Israel and the followers of Christ, Jesus will return from heaven with His saints to quickly defeat the forces of evil. "I saw heaven standing open and there before me was a white horse, whose rider is called Faithful and True [Jesus]. With justice he judges and makes war. [12] His eyes are like blazing fire, and on his head are many crowns. He has a name written on him that no one knows but he himself. [13] He is dressed in a robe dipped in blood, and his name is the Word of God. [14] The armies of heaven were following him, riding on white horses and dressed in fine linen, white and clean. [15] Out of his mouth comes a sharp sword with which to strike down the nations" (Rev 19:11-15).

- Jesus will then set up His Millennial Kingdom on earth. This is a beautiful time of peace and harmony on earth, lasting one thousand years. The saints will reign with Christ during this time. "He will rule them with an iron scepter. He treads the winepress of the fury of the wrath of God Almighty. [16] On his robe and on his thigh he has this name written: KING OF KINGS and LORD OF LORDS" (Rev 19:15-16).

  "They came to life and reigned with Christ a thousand years" (Rev 20:4).

- At the conclusion of this thousand year period, God will set up the final heaven and earth. All those who have chosen to follow Jesus will spend their eternity with Him in perfect peace, joy, and harmony. The Bible also says that those who have rejected Jesus, will be judged at the Great White Throne judgment and spend their eternity separated from God. "Now I saw a new heaven and a new earth, for the first heaven and the first earth had passed away... [2] Then I, John, saw the holy city, New Jerusalem, coming down out of heaven from God, prepared as a bride adorned for her husband. [3] And I heard a loud voice from heaven saying, "Behold, the tabernacle of God is with men, and He will dwell with them, and they shall be His people. God Himself will be with them and be their God. [4] And God will wipe away every tear from their eyes; there shall be no more death, nor sorrow, nor crying. There shall be no more pain, for the former things have passed away" (Rev 21:1-4).

Many of the details of the coming end-time events have been omitted in the description above. However, enough have been summarized to allow the reader to understand how each of the fifty signs of the end times will lead to the coming Rapture and subsequent seven year Tribulation. For anyone who desires to learn a little more about the biblical prophecies concerning the coming Tribulation, please see Appendix 1.

As it turns out, most of the signs given in the Bible concerning the end times relate to the time of the Tribulation. Given my belief that the Rapture will occur just before the Tribulation begins, how can one use the events that will occur during the Tribulation to determine the times in which we now live? We certainly are not currently living in that terrible time of God's great wrath. The answer may well be gleaned from an understanding of the manner by which God has generally worked His providential care of this world since the time of Adam. All throughout history, God rarely intervened to change the course of history in a *blatantly supernatural* way. However, I do believe that God has influenced and changed the course of history through His direct involvement on many occasions. Scores of biblical examples testify to this.

For example, although the brothers of Joseph meant harm when they sold him into slavery, God meant this act of betrayal for good. After rising to the position of Prime Minister of Egypt, thereby allowing him to help his family (and many others) during a time of severe famine in the land, Joseph explained, "But God sent me ahead of you to preserve for you a remnant on earth and to save your lives by a great deliverance. [8] **So then it was not you that sent me here, but God**. He made me father to Pharaoh, lord of his entire household, and ruler of all Egypt" (Gen 45:7-8). Consider also the plagues God visited on Egypt during the time of Moses and how that resulted in the freeing of the Jews. Never forget the sacrificial death of God's Son, Jesus, on the cross to save those who place their trust in Him. God has also acted, at times, to alter His natural laws, like when He protected Shadrach, Meschak and Abednego from the fire, when Jesus turned water into wine and walked on water, and when Moses parted the Red Sea.

However, never do I recall God using His supernatural powers to *totally usurp the natural physical laws of His universe to transform a significant portion of land, sea or humanity.* Although God certainly does use His infinite power and knowledge to direct the events of earth and mankind, He does it by using short episodes of blatant miracles and by influencing man to act according to His will in other cases. I truly believe that God works in a powerful, mysterious providential manner to bring about His will for humanity and this world.

God rarely seems to override natural laws to effect grand and long lasting changes of earth's topography or other aspects of nature. For example, it is doubtful that we will ever see thousands of people walking across the ocean or witness an entire city disappear overnight. God does not currently work that way on a large scale, nor has He since the Creation.

Because of this, people should understand that if certain events are going to occur during the Tribulation, and this seven year period begins very soon after the Rapture, one would expect the ground work for some of these things to begin before the Rapture. For example, if the Third Temple exists during the Tribulation (and it does), it is quite likely that the Jews would be at least planning on building it in the years leading up to the Rapture. This is not absolutely necessary as God is sovereign and can accomplish any non-contradictory task that He desires. However, as just explained, it is highly unlikely that He would use His creative power to suddenly "speak" this Temple into existence soon after the Rapture. Therefore, it is reasonable to believe that *there will be many signs leading up to the Rapture relating directly to those events that are seen just after it occurs.* Interestingly, many of these signs have now made themselves manifest.

In fact, fifty signs of the end times will be presented in the chapters that follow. They will include those noted in both the Old and the New Testaments. The evidence for these events having become manifest in recent history will be discussed. I believe that it will become clearly evident that there has never been a time in all of world history where so many of these signs have come together as the times in which we currently live. I suggest that it is likely Jesus will rapture His saints within the next twenty or thirty years, possibly much sooner. Of course, it is conceivable that He could come for His church while you are reading these words since the Bible does make clear that His return could happen at any time.

The following discussion of the "signs of the end times" will be divided into three major subject areas:

- Those prophecies related directly to the nation and people of Israel, God's chosen people.
- End-time prophetic verses that relate to other nations and people of the world – coming from both the Old and New Testaments.
- The Olivet Discourse, where the Lord Jesus detailed the events that the world would experience just prior to His Second Coming.

There is no doubt that even non-Christians sense that there are many eerie things happening in our world today. As will be shown, many Muslims believe that the end of this age is coming soon. Given the terrible famine and pestilence in recent decades, the increase in chemical and biological warfare, and, especially, the relatively easy availability of nuclear weapons in our time, even secularists worry that an event such as nuclear winter might one day in the decades just ahead bring the world to a cataclysmic end.

Therefore, many believe that there is no hope for humanity. Fortunately, those with this pessimistic outlook are wrong. It is important to note that the Holy Bible, God's Word, tells us that the world will never end. Yes, there will be a new age coming. Not the new age some believe will be brought to earth by human effort – that will never come to pass. However, one day in the not too distant future, the Lord of this universe will once again return to earth, defeat the forces of evil, and usher in a beautiful Messianic Age, known as the Millennial Kingdom. This will lead ultimately into the final heaven and earth where all those who have placed their trust in Jesus will spend their eternity.

God has given us excellent evidence that He is the loving Creator of this universe. God has also demonstrated that all of His prophecies are true. Given the precise fulfillment of hundreds of past prophecies, we can be sure that His prophecies of this future glorious kingdom age will also come to pass. His Son, Jesus, will come one day in the near future. Until that time, He has asked His followers to take heed of the signs of the times and remember that... "When these things begin to take place, stand up and lift up your heads, because your redemption is drawing near" (Luke 21:28).

Section 1:

GOD WILL RESTORE ISRAEL IN THE END TIMES

THERE IS NO more important and impressive series of fulfilled prophecy in all of eschatology than the amazing events that have befallen the nation of Israel in the last sixty-five years. In fact, the recent restoration of Israel as a nation is the major reason that most biblical prophecy teachers are so convinced that the Rapture of the church cannot be very far off in the future. In the first section of this book, many of the end-time prophecies relating to the nation and people of Israel will be studied.

Interestingly, the Bible does say that the majority of the signs of the last days will relate to the Jews, God's chosen people. There is absolutely no doubt that Israel rejected God and His Laws in the past. Therefore, the Jewish people received their just punishment from a Holy God. He allowed their nation to be conquered by the Assyrians and the Babylonians. This rejection of God also resulted in the Diaspora... the scattering of the Jews around the world for multiple millennia.

However, God also made many wonderful and irrevocable covenants with Israel which He has every intention of keeping.

Virtually all of the end-time signs that concern Israel and the Jews relate to His fulfillment of these Old Testament promises. The exciting aspect of this study is the fact that all of these end-time promises have already been completely fulfilled or are just at the cusp of final realization. No other period in history has witnessed such an amazing number and array of end-time prophecies fulfilled.

For example, God said that He would one day bring His chosen people back to their Promised Land from all parts of the world and re-establish their nation. Israel had no nation to call their own for over two thousand years. Then, in May 1948, God providentially restored the Jews to their original Promised Land as an independent nation. God also said that after this regathering, He would richly bless their land. Prior to the return of the Jews, Palestine was only a vast desert wasteland, but God honored His promise and proceeded to mightily bless the land. Another example concerns the Third Temple. This Temple must be ready for occupancy during the Tribulation. No realistic thought had ever been given to rebuilding this Temple until recent decades. God also promised that He would protect Israel during the many wars of the end times. Of course, this promise made no sense until Israel became a united nation again. These are just a few of the many events that are exclusively taking place in our time that demonstrate God's fulfillment of end-times prophecy.

Let us now take a more detailed look at the many intriguing latter day signs affecting Israel. God is using these signs of the times to make it very apparent that His Son will soon return.

Chapter 1

GOD WILL REGATHER HIS CHOSEN
PEOPLE IN THE LATTER DAYS

THE MOST IMPORTANT end-time prophecies relate to the regathering of the nation and people of Israel. There are very few prophecy teachers who would argue this point. Throughout the early portion of the Old Testament, known to the Jews as the Torah, God repeatedly covenanted with the patriarchs that He would bless them if they followed His edicts, but curse them if they rebelled. Unfortunately for the Israelites of that time, they usually chose not to follow God. Eventually, God allowed His chosen people to receive the just punishment for their transgressions. The Northern Kingdom, referred to as Israel, followed by the Southern Kingdom, Judah, were both defeated in battle. Their people were killed, taken captive, or exiled to the far corners of the earth.

However, even with Israel abandoned and the Jews scattered around the world, God still had many covenants to keep. How would God keep any of these promises given the situation that existed following the fall of Jerusalem in A.D. 70? The situation continued to decline when Hadrian defeated, disbanded, and even renamed Jerusalem and Israel in A.D. 135. Israel, abandoned by God and scattered about the world, did not seem a likely candidate for the reunification into a cohesive nation as God had promised.

Despite any apparent difficulties, God has kept His promise in impressive fashion.

This chapter will show how God brought the Jews from all around the four corners of the globe back into their Promised Land. There is no longer any animosity between Israel and Judah. Jerusalem once again has become their capital. Even their ancient language of Hebrew has been restored. God has shown Israel and the world that He will always honor His covenants. The most important date in current Israeli history is May 14, 1948. Let us now see why.

1. Israel Will Become a Nation Once Again:

The nation of Israel ceased to exist after the Assyrians defeated its northern kingdom in 722 B.C., and its southern kingdom, Judah, became a vassal state to Nebuchadnezzar in 605 B.C. By 586 B.C., Jerusalem and its beautiful First Temple had been destroyed. Since that time, the Jews have had no land to call their own. Over the centuries, the vast majority of Jewish people dispersed throughout the world - as predicted in the Old Testament. After their resounding defeat by the Romans in A.D. 70, they no longer had the Second Temple in which to worship and were effectively evacuated from Jerusalem by the victors. In A.D. 135, Roman Emperor Hadrian abolished the names of Judea and Samaria, creating the new name of Palestine for the region in an attempt to erase any memory of the Jewish race. Jerusalem was renamed Aelia Capitolina for the same reason. However, Hadrian's scheme of ethnic cleansing against the Jews was not going to succeed as God had other plans. On the other hand, this action against the Jews has caused many problems over the centuries, especially today, as there are now a group of non-Jewish people who have adopted the name "Palestinians" to help them in their cause. As is now common knowledge, these Palestinians want as much of the current land of Israel as they can get. Unfortunately, far too many of the Arab neighbors of Israel also

14

have as their goal to rid the world of the Jews. Let us see what the Bible says is the ultimate fate of the "Promised Land"...

The hand of the LORD was upon me, and **he brought me out by the Spirit of the Lord and set me in the middle of a valley; it was full of bones.** ² He led me back and forth among them, and I saw a great many bones on the floor of the valley, **bones that were very dry.** ³ He asked me, "Son of man, can these bones live?" I said, "O Sovereign LORD, you alone know." ⁴ Then he said to me, "Prophesy to these bones and say to them, **'Dry bones, hear the word of the Lord!** ⁵ This is what the Sovereign LORD says to these bones: **I will make breath enter you, and you will come to life.** ⁶ I will attach tendons to you and make flesh come upon you and cover you with skin; I will put breath in you, and you will come to life. Then you will know that I am the LORD.'" ⁷ So I prophesied as I was commanded. And as I was prophesying, there was a noise, a rattling sound, and the bones came together, bone to bone. ⁸ I looked, and tendons and flesh appeared on them and skin covered them, but there was no breath in them. ⁹ Then he said to me, "Prophesy to the breath; prophesy, son of man, and say to it, 'This is what the Sovereign LORD says: Come from the four winds, O breath, and breathe into these slain, that they may live.'" ¹⁰ So I prophesied as he commanded me, and breath entered them; they came to life and stood up on their feet--a vast army. ¹¹ Then he said to me: **"Son of man, these bones are the whole house of Israel.** They say, 'Our bones are dried up and our hope is gone; we are cut off.' ¹² Therefore prophesy and say to them: 'This is what the Sovereign LORD says: O my people, I am going to open your graves and bring you up from them; **I will bring you back to the land of Israel.** ¹³ **Then you, my people, will know that I am the Lord,** when I open your graves and bring you up from them. ¹⁴ **I will put my Spirit in you and you will live, and I will settle you in your own land.** Then you will know that I the LORD have spoken, and I have done it, declares the LORD.'" (Ezek 37:1-14)

"For **this is what the Sovereign Lord says: I myself will search for my sheep and look after them.** ¹² As a shepherd looks after his scattered flock when he is with them, so will I look after my sheep. **I will rescue them from all the places where they were scattered** on a day of clouds and darkness. ¹³ **I will bring them out from the nations and gather them from the countries, and I will bring them into their own land. I will pasture them on the mountains of Israel**, in the ravines and in all the settlements in the land. ¹⁴ I will tend them in a good pasture, and the mountain heights of Israel will be their grazing land. There they will lie down in good grazing land, and there they will feed in a rich pasture on the mountains of Israel." (Ezek 34:11-14)

"The days are coming," declares the LORD, "when **I will bring my people Israel and Judah back from captivity and restore them to the land I gave their forefathers** to possess," says the LORD. (Jer 30:3)

"I will bring them from the land of the north and gather them from the ends of the earth. Among them will be the blind and the lame, expectant mothers and women in labor; a great throng will return. ⁹ They will come with weeping; they will pray as I bring them back." (Jer 31:8-9)

"At that time I will gather you; at that time I will bring you home. I will give you honor and praise among all the peoples of the earth when I restore your fortunes before your very eyes," says the LORD. (Zeph 3:20)

These five verse selections detail God's final regathering of the Jews from the four corners of the earth. There are many similar verses concerning God's plan for Israel in the end times. As the latter days approach, the Bible states that God will once again reunite His chosen people in the land of their fathers. After many centuries lying dormant, Israel will once again rise from the ashes. As Ezekiel suggests in his parable of the "dry bones," Israel was "dead" for all that time – physically there was no nation, and spiritually, the people, as a whole, were out of harmony with God. They had rejected Him.

Then, on May 14, 1948, Israel became a nation once again. This was quite a remarkable occurrence. In fact, it was totally unique in human history. Never before had a nation of people with its own specific identity been defeated and scattered throughout the world for such a long period of time (in this case it was for over two thousand years) only to come together as a nation again – as the rightful heirs of that land. Yet, God said that it would happen near the time of the return of His Son, and it has happened. There was a tremendous amount of political haggling involved in this return of national status to Israel. Great Britain had exercised control over the Palestinian territories since the conclusion of World War I. The League of Nations had given Britain this authority in June of 1922 via a treaty known as the British Mandate. The newly formed United Nations was balking at their promise to restore a homeland for the Jews after World War II. However, the leadership of the Jewish people was resolute in their plan to regain their national status as the British Mandate wound to a conclusion. Therefore, on May 14, 1948, the Jews declared their national independence and named their "new" nation, Israel. This was to take effect when the mandate ceased to exist at midnight that same day. Not surprisingly, as Isaiah prophesied, this nation came about suddenly, in one day. "Who has ever heard of such a thing? Who has ever seen such things? **Can a country be born in a day** or a nation be brought forth in a moment? Yet no sooner is Zion in labor than she gives birth to her children" (Isaiah 66:8). The United States, to their credit, recognized Israel's statehood. However, war with many of their Arab neighbors was

17

almost immediately required to finally cement this historic event. Israel, despite long odds, won this war for their independence. This was to be the first of many wars that would be required to keep their nation intact.

During the last century, millions of Jews migrated back to their rightful homeland from all over the earth. Just as Ezekiel wrote, they came from the north (e.g., Russia), south (e.g., Africa), east (e.g., many different Muslim countries) and west (e.g., United States).

> "Now learn this lesson from the fig tree: As soon as its twigs get tender and its leaves come out, you know that summer is near." (Matt 24:32)

This quote from Jesus came from His Olivet Discourse immediately after telling His disciples about the signs of His coming. Some see this statement by the Lord Jesus as a general affirmation that His return should be expected soon after certain specific events begin to occur on the earth. Many prophecy scholars interpret this verse in a more specific manner. They believe that Jesus is using the fig tree as a symbol for Israel in this parable. It is typically used in just that way throughout the Scriptures. If that is the case here, Jesus is saying that soon after Israel becomes a nation once again and begins to grow and develop (i.e., the tender branch is putting out leaves), it is to be understood that He will soon thereafter return to rapture His church into heaven.

Mark Hitchcock, in his recent book, *The Amazing Claims of Bible Prophecy*, pointed out that noted preacher J.C. Ryle wrote in the mid-nineteenth century how he was amazed that only the Jew was able to retain their national identity while being scattered throughout the entire world for the past two thousand years. No other dispersed national population has ever been able to make this claim. This was one hundred years before they once again had a nation to call their own. Hitchcock went on to quote Dr. Randall

Price, "The modern return of the Jewish people to the Land of Israel has been called the 'Miracle of the Mediterranean.' Such a return by a people group that had been scattered is unprecedented in history. Indeed, the Jewish people are the only exiled people to remain a distinct people despite being dispersed to more than 70 different countries for more than 20 centuries. The mighty empires of Egypt, Assyria, Babylon, Persia, Greece, and Rome all ravaged their land, took their people captive, and scattered them throughout the earth. Even after this, they suffered persecution, pogrom [i.e., organized massacre], and Holocaust in the lands to which they were exiled. Yet, all of these ancient kingdoms have turned to dust and their former glories remain only as museum relics and many of the nations that opposed the Jews have suffered economic, political, or religious decline. But the Jewish people whom they enslaved and tried to eradicate live free and have again become a strong nation." [1]

Let me make one final point on this topic. Ezekiel noted in his vision of the "dry bones" that first these bones would come to life. This has happened. Next, this living body would soon receive the Spirit of God. That has not yet happened to any significant degree. However, during the Tribulation, God will indeed pour out His Spirit into this newly alive entity. The Jewish people, who have recently returned to Israel in droves, will then turn back to God through their newfound belief in Jesus. They will finally recognize Jesus as their true Messiah.

2. Judah and Israel Reunite:

After Solomon died, the United Kingdom of Israel was divided. This resulted in a Northern Kingdom and a Southern Kingdom. The Southern Kingdom, which included Jerusalem, was called Judah and was composed primarily of the tribes of Judah and Benjamin. Most of the tribe of Levi also lived in the Southern Kingdom as their priestly duties involved the Temple which was located in Jerusalem. The Northern Kingdom, named Israel, was composed of the remaining ten tribes. These two kingdoms remained separate for several hundred years. Finally, both were conquered by foreign invasions and their people scattered from their respective homelands. The Lord promised to reunite the entire nation of Israel in the end times...

> **In that day the Lord will reach out his hand a second time to reclaim the remnant that is left of his people** ... **He will raise a banner for the nations and gather the exiles of Israel; he will assemble the scattered people of Judah from the four quarters of the earth.** [13] Ephraim's [Israel's] jealousy will vanish, and Judah's enemies will be cut off; **Ephraim will not be jealous of Judah, nor Judah hostile toward Ephraim.** (Isaiah 11:11,12-13)

> Again the word of the LORD came to me, saying, [16] "As for you, son of man, **take a stick for yourself** and write on it: 'For **Judah** and for the children of Israel, his companions.' Then take another stick and write on it, 'For **Joseph, the stick of Ephraim**, and for all the house of Israel, his companions.' [17] Then **join them one to another for yourself into one stick, and they will become one in your hand."** (Ezek 37:15-17)

> **"This is what the Sovereign Lord says**: I am going to take the stick of Joseph--which is in Ephraim's hand--and of the Israelite tribes associated with him, and join it to Judah's stick, making them a single stick of wood, and **they will become one in my hand."** (Ezek 37:19)

Ezekiel prophesied about these two kingdoms, Israel (represented by the stick of Ephraim or Joseph) and Judah. This prophecy came immediately after his prophecy concerning the restoration of the nation of Israel in the latter days.

The Northern Kingdom (Israel) lasted only two hundred years before God allowed Assyria to conquer it and its people as punishment for their sins. The Southern Kingdom (Judah) lasted somewhat longer, but eventually God brought the Babylonians in to teach them about the consequences of rejecting Him and His edicts. King Nebuchadnezzar defeated Judah and destroyed Jerusalem and its Temple. He also brought many Jewish slaves back with him into captivity. Although there were many thousands of Jews who did return to their homeland many years later, most did not.

However, God had no intention of letting His chosen people languish forever in foreign lands. He had made promises to Abraham, Isaac, Jacob, and David. God never breaks a promise. Therefore, not only have we seen God arrange human events to bring the Jews from all over the world back to their homeland, but He has also reunited the divided kingdoms of Israel and Judah. Currently, there certainly is no separation between the tribes in Israel. All of the Jews live in relative harmony in Israel today.

3. Jerusalem Becomes Part of Israel Again:

> "On that day I will make the leaders of Judah like a firepot in a woodpile, like a flaming torch among sheaves. They will consume right and left all the surrounding peoples, but **Jerusalem will remain intact in her place.**" (Zech 12:6)

> For the LORD will rebuild Zion (Jerusalem) and appear in his glory. (Psalms 102:16)

> "They will fall by the sword, and will be taken as prisoners to all the nations. **Jerusalem will be trampled on by Gentiles until the times of the Gentiles are fulfilled.**" (Luke 21:24)

In the first quote above, Zechariah stated that in the end times Jerusalem would be inhabited by the Jews once again. The psalmist noted that the Lord would one day rebuild Jerusalem just prior to

His glorious return. Therefore, it was of prophetic interest that a major result of the famous "Six-Day War" in 1967 was the fact that Israel once again regained control of the city of Jerusalem. It is now that nation's capital city.

Jesus noted in His Olivet Discourse that the Jews would not regain permanent control of Jerusalem until the time of the Gentiles was fulfilled. Given the situation today, the time of the Gentiles being "fulfilled" would appear to be just over the horizon. Unfortunately, it is still the case that many nations continue to bicker about the rightful ownership of this city. This issue will not be totally resolved until the return of Jesus when He will defeat Satan and his forces in the Battle of Armageddon. Even so, there is still no doubt that almost one million Jews live in their capital city, just as the prophet Zechariah said would be the case in the last days.

4. The Ancient Language of Hebrew Returns:

The ancient Jews spoke the Hebrew language. However, even by the time of Christ, this language had ceased to exist in everyday usage. After the Assyrians defeated the Northern Kingdom of Israel in 722 B.C., those ten tribes of Jews were scattered throughout the surrounding territories and beyond. A little over one hundred years later, the Babylonians defeated Judah and took tens of thousands of their defeated foes as slaves and workers back to their own country. The remainder migrated off to places such as Egypt. In any event, virtually all of these chosen people had to adopt the language of their new homelands. Aramaic, and later, Greek, became the language of the masses. Only the Levite priests continued to use Hebrew by the time the Second Temple was built. They felt Hebrew was important to use in their Temple ceremonies. Five hundred years later, the language of the Jews, even those living in Israel, was either Aramaic, Greek, or Latin.

Yet, God had plans for His chosen people to not only return to their allotted land, but also to once again speak in their old Hebrew language. Note what God stated through His prophet Zephaniah during the days of the building of the Second Temple, "For then I will restore to the peoples a pure language, that they all may call on the name of the LORD, to serve Him with one accord" (Zeph 3:9, NKJV).

Some prophecy scholars do not interpret this verse to mean a pure language in the sense that Jews would once again speak Hebrew. However, many modern prophecy teachers do believe that this is what was meant by the Holy Spirit who spoke through the prophet Zephaniah over 2,500 years ago. In any case, it is quite an incredible fact that after totally dying out of common usage for thousands of years, the original Hebrew language of Israel has returned as a spoken language for God's chosen people, the Jews.

Eliezer Ben-Yehuda was the man responsible for bringing back Hebrew as the language of the masses in Israel today. He stated in the late nineteenth century, "The Hebrew language can live only if we revive the nation and return it to the fatherland."[2] As a corollary, he also noted that a return to the use of their original language would be one stimulus to help bring Jews back from around the world to their common homeland. He was correct in this assumption. His life story is very interesting.

At the age of twelve, Ben-Yehuda said that he had a vision where he saw light flash across the sky and a voice spoke three times saying, "The land and the language." He took this as a sign from God that he was to restore Hebrew as the common language in the land of the Jews... Israel. Of course, there was no Israel at that time. Many years would pass. As a young adult, he contracted tuberculosis while studying medicine in Paris. One day, while recovering from this dreaded disease, he once again heard the call, "The land and the language." This second visitation from God, as Ben-Yehuda interpreted it, resulted in his dedicating the remaining years of his life to the task of developing the Hebrew language for common usage in Jewish Palestine, and later, in Israel. His crowning work was a seventeen volume lexicon/dictionary of the Hebrew language. Despite enduring a life of severe persecution (even to members of his family), he lived to see Hebrew recognized as the official language of the Palestinian Jews beginning in 1922, just one month before his death. The restoration of this ancient language into general usage today in Israel serves as one of the more impressive fulfilled biblical prophecies concerning the end times. There is no other example like this in world history.[3]

5. The Ethiopian Jews Will Return Prior to the Return of Christ:

During the time of Solomon, a significant number of Jews migrated to Ethiopia with Prince Menelik, the son of Solomon born to the Queen of Sheba. Members of each of the twelve tribes of Israel accompanied him upon his return. Zephaniah, approximately 400 years later, prophesied that in the latter days, these Ethiopian Jews would return to Israel once again. "From beyond the rivers of Cush [**Ethiopia**] my worshipers, my scattered people, will bring me offerings" (Zeph 3:10).

The prophet Isaiah also had something to say about the Ethiopian contingent of the Diaspora (i.e., the scattering of the Jews from their homeland). He said that Jews would one day return to their ancestral home from all points of the earth, including the south. Of course, Ethiopia is south of Israel. "I will bring your children from the east, and gather you from the west; [6]I will say to the north, 'Give them up!' **And to the *south*, 'Do not hold them back!' Bring my sons from afar, and my daughters from the ends of the earth**" (Isaiah 43:5-6).

In 1991, the sitting Ethiopian government was in danger of being toppled by rebel forces. This placed the Jews in that nation in grave danger. The Israeli government quickly put a daring evacuation plan into action. Over 14,300 Ethiopian "Falasha" Jews were airlifted home to Israel in a wonderful example of the coordinated efforts of several Jewish organizations and the Israeli government to rescue their fellow Jewish brothers and sisters from a possible holocaust. Incredibly, this "Operation Solomon" was accomplished in only thirty-six hours using thirty-four planes.

In two earlier missions, "Operation Moses" and "Operation Joshua," over 8,000 Ethiopian Jews from late 1984 to early 1985 were rescued through another coordinated effort, this time, by the governments of Israel and United States. Thousands of Jews from Ethiopia fled by foot into refugee camps in Sudan. Unfortunately, as many as 4,000 died during that journey. However, once they made it into Sudan, the refugees were taken safely to Israel.

The point is that thousands of Jews from Ethiopia have recently been brought back to Israel as prophesied in the Old Testament Scriptures. God is bringing His chosen people home from all parts of the globe in these latter days.

Chapter 2

ISRAEL, THE WORLD, AND THE MESSIAH

AFTER GOD brings Jews from all around the globe back to their homeland in the latter days, the Gentile nations of the world will take notice. In fact, the vast majority of the world will be very much against their return. Their age-old enemies, the Arabs, will always cause trouble for Israel. The most important city in the world, Jerusalem, will be the center of attention. Although, God has given this city to the Jews, most of the world does not see it this way. For this reason, the Bible says that Jerusalem will be fought over by many nations. Until the Messiah comes to rule and reign with power, the nation of Israel will be divided as well.

The Bible also makes it clear that when the Jews first return to their land and reclaim their nation and capital, they will not have turned back to God in faith. In fact, God will use this time as well as the time of the Tribulation, to convince the Jews that Jesus is the Messiah. Until they recognize this truth, Israel will be primarily a secular society with a democratic form of government.

At some point soon after His Second Coming, Jesus will walk through the Eastern Gate of the city as He walks to the Temple. Until that time, the prophet Ezekiel wrote, this special gate will remain sealed. Of course, after His return, Jesus will be recognized as Messiah and King for all eternity.

6. Jerusalem Will Be Fought Over by Many Nations:

> "I am going to make Jerusalem a cup that sends all the surrounding peoples reeling. Judah will be besieged as well as Jerusalem. ³ On *that day*, when all the nations of the earth are gathered against her, I will make Jerusalem an immovable rock for all the nations. All who try to move it will injure themselves." (Zech 12:2-3)

As the preceding verses show, the possession of Jerusalem will be at the center of international turmoil as the time for Christ's return draws near (i.e., in *"that day"*). Zechariah was writing concerning the end times when he wrote the words above. It is worth noting that, until these last sixty years, Jerusalem has certainly not been an "immovable rock for all the nations." There have been many times in history that this city of God has been fought over, but only at this time can it truthfully be stated that Jerusalem has become a "cup that sends all the surrounding peoples reeling." It is quite obvious that Jerusalem is the most fought over city in the world at this time. The world news reports on the conflict over Jerusalem almost daily.

The fate of Jerusalem, therefore, has gained the attention of the world. When Israel became a nation once again in May 1948 and until 1967, the city of Jerusalem still remained divided. This great city has seen the use of such things as barbed-wire fences and walls to divide it into Jewish and Palestinian regions. During the twenty years from 1948 to 1967, the Jewish Quarter with its synagogues was destroyed. Graves and monuments were desecrated. It was not until the 1967 Six-Day War that Jerusalem and the Temple Mount were liberated. On June 7 of that year, Israeli troops stood at the Western Wall and Rabbi Shlomo Goren declared, "We have taken the city of God. We are entering the Messianic era for the Jewish people, and I promise to the Christian world that what we are responsible for we will take care of."

Unfortunately, on June 17, 1967, Israeli Defense Minister Moshe Dayan, a secular Jew, gave back control of the Temple Mount to the Supreme Muslim Council. Amazingly, this Israeli was quoted as saying, "We must view the Temple Mount as a historic site relating to past memory." How could he forget the vast history of the Temple Mount that related to David, Solomon, and even to God Himself? The top of the Temple Mount was given over to the Muslims to administer. Today no non-Muslim worship or archaeological activity is allowed on the Temple Mount.

As never before in history, Jerusalem is at the center of today's headlines. The city which grew up around the small walled village captured by King David from the Jebusites three thousand years ago is the focal point of never-ending debate among the great superpowers. It is a fact that no other city in the world is fought over and discussed more than the "City of David"... Jerusalem. This has truly been the case throughout all history. Jerusalem has been fought over by armies of the Assyrians, Babylonians, Egyptians, Greeks, Ptolemies, Seleucids, Romans, Byzantines, Persians, Arabs, Crusaders, Mongols, the Turks, Britain, Syria, and Jordan. Today the United States, the United Nations, Israel, and the Palestinian leadership are almost constantly working to determine a peaceful way to divide Jerusalem between Israel and the Muslim Palestinians. This is not going to happen, ultimately.

God states that this city is actually meant for Him. Jerusalem will be where His Son, Jesus, will reign during the Millennial Kingdom. It also becomes obvious after reading the prophecies of the latter days, that Israel will retain possession once they have regained it... as they did in 1967. Of course, this is not to say that they will not have to fend off many aggressors over the years.

Prime Minister Benjamin Netanyahu has boldly stated that he has no intention of giving control of any additional portion of Jerusalem to any other people or nation. The Roman Catholic Church has always had very strong interests in that city. The

Vatican's legal adviser, David Jaeger, recently was quoted as saying that "Jerusalem is an important city, the fate of which should not be left in the hands of Israel and the Palestinians."[4] Evangelical Christians are taught, appropriately, to always pray for the peace of Jerusalem. It is the birthplace of Christianity. The Muslim nations have no intention of allowing Jews to have any lasting control over what they perceive as one of their holiest cities. In other words, the Jews, Christians, and Muslims all consider Jerusalem as very important to their religious heritage. A stalemate has been in existence for decades now. Eventually, the Scriptures tell us, enemy nations will come against Israel in war once again to decide the fate of Israel and its capital city. Given the course of political events and the many signs of the soon coming of Jesus, it would appear that this great time of Tribulation is not far off in the future.

As we shall see, during the seven year Tribulation, the veracity of this prophecy will become even more evident as nation after nation will turn their attention to Jerusalem with every intention of expelling the Jews. However, God will intervene, and Israel will continue to defeat its enemies. God will not let that great city fall the next time it faces destruction… if, indeed, we are in the end times.

It is very interesting, even miraculous, that Israel was triumphant in the battles against their warring neighbors in 1948, 1967 and 1973. Logic would have strongly suggested that they should have lost every one of those wars… and overwhelmingly so. It really is a worthwhile experience to read about these wars to see the "hand" of God upon Israel as He providentially worked His wonders to direct the final outcome. In another sign of the end times to be discussed later, some amazing examples of a few of the miracles seen in those wars will be described. God will certainly protect Israel and Jerusalem in the coming years.

> On that day [the end times] the LORD will shield those
> who live in Jerusalem, so that the feeblest among them

will be like David, and **the house of David will be like God, like the Angel of the Lord going before them. [9] On that day I will set out to destroy all the nations that attack Jerusalem.** (Zech 12:8-9)

7. Jerusalem Will Be An Unwalled City in the Last Days:

You will say, "**I will invade a land of unwalled villages;** I will attack a peaceful and unsuspecting people--all of them living without walls and without gates and bars. [12] I will plunder and loot and turn my hand against the resettled ruins and the people gathered from the nations, rich in livestock and goods, living at the center of the land." (Ezek 38:11-12)

"Jerusalem shall be inhabited as towns without walls." (Zech 2:4)

Ezekiel and Zechariah both wrote of the time just prior to the return of Jesus when Jerusalem will once again be occupied by the Jews. The regathering by God will result in a well-populated city. The interesting thing, however, is that the city will no longer be protected by the walls that were so necessary in the times during which these prophets lived. Although this prophecy must have seemed odd to those two great men as they wrote it down, it has certainly come true today.

Modern Jerusalem, as is true of virtually all modern cities, does not have a wall surrounding it for protection from foreign invaders. This would not have been easy for a man to foresee when this prediction was made over 2,500 years ago. In fact, it would have made no sense at all. Of course, a man did not predict this... it was a prophecy from God.

In the days when this prophecy was written, all cities of any note were protected by fortified walls. This was true of Jerusalem.

Remember, Nehemiah was allowed to return to his homeland for the express purpose of rebuilding the walls, as it was such a critically important item for the city's defense. However, even though Ezekiel had just prophesied that Jerusalem was going to be attacked by many surrounding nations, he followed up that prophecy with the one about the city of Jerusalem not having any fortifying walls around its borders. Why in the world would that be the case? The answer today is obvious. Walls would be of no real value in this day of airplanes and missiles and artillery. Other methods of defense have long since replaced the city wall. God, of course, was privy to this knowledge; only God would have known about this twenty-five hundred years ago.

8. Jerusalem Rebuilt in Nine Specific Directions:

> "The days are coming," declares the LORD, "when this city [Jerusalem] will be rebuilt for me **from the Tower of Hananel to the Corner Gate.** [39] The measuring line will stretch **from there straight to the hill of Gareb and then turn to Goah.** [40] The whole valley where dead bodies and ashes are thrown, and all the terraces **out to the Kidron Valley on the east as far as the corner of the Horse Gate**, will be holy to the LORD. **The city will never again be uprooted or demolished.**" (Jer 31:38-40)

> The whole land, from Geba to Rimmon, south of Jerusalem, will become like the Arabah [desert plain]. But Jerusalem will be raised up and remain in its place, from the Benjamin Gate to the site of the First Gate, to the Corner Gate, and from the Tower of Hananel to the royal winepresses. [11] **It will be inhabited; never again will it be destroyed. Jerusalem will be secure.** (Zech 14:10-11)

Jeremiah and Zechariah were very specific about how the Holy City of Jerusalem was going to be rebuilt in the last days. In particular, each of these great prophets wrote that once Jerusalem was rebuilt in the end times, it would never again be destroyed. We have seen in recent decades just how important Israel and its capital are to God.

God also gave Jeremiah the specific order in which the various sections of the Holy City would be rebuilt. The terminology is foreign to the reader of this day. However, there are Jewish historians who have been able to show just how, once again, another of God's prophecies has been fulfilled literally and completely.

Although not all prophecy scholars agree on the significance of this sign, it is worth noting that one of the more important apologists of the last half of the twentieth century, Josh McDowell, was convinced that the order in which Jerusalem was recently rebuilt was, in fact, an impressive fulfillment of Old Testament prophecy. McDowell wrote on this topic extensively in his groundbreaking book, *Evidence that Demands a Verdict*. He quoted writer, George Davis who wrote, "It would be difficult to quote a Bible prophecy that is more definite and graphic than is this forecast by Jeremiah of the oft-destroyed city of Jerusalem."[5] Then Josh went on to say, "Jeremiah uses clear landmarks to chart the route of the unusual growth of this city. These guide posts have remained many centuries until some of them were destroyed due to city growth, i.e., the fulfillment of the prophecy."[6] McDowell then proceeded to explain, point by point, just how the actual growth of Jerusalem has followed the course prophesied by the prophets 2,500 years ago. He concluded this discussion by noting that, "The growth of the city has not covered the prescribed route of growth, but has followed, point by point, the line set down by Jeremiah. The prophet told a step-by-step progression of the growth of Jerusalem, and this process has been followed in actual fact with closeness. There are other prophecies dealing with the southward trends of growth which have also been systematically fulfilled."[7]

A Jerusalem professor, Peter Stoner, also wrote in his book *Science Speaks: An Evaluation of Certain Christian Evidences* that "nine items were named in the expansion of the city of Jerusalem. First, it was prophesied that it would expand, then the order of expansion."[8] Stoner then calculated the odds of rebuilding the city in the manner and order written by Jeremiah. He arrived at a figure of one chance in eighty billion. I do believe that Dr. Stoner went a little overboard in his assessment as he was trying to prove his point that only God could forecast something so unlikely as this… and then have it come true so literally. On the other hand, Jeremiah's prophecy was definitely quite specific and multifaceted on the matter of how Jerusalem was going to be rebuilt. The fact is, according to several Jewish historians, it absolutely has come true.

9. Israel Will Be Partitioned by Other Nations.

> "In those days and at that time, when I restore the fortunes of Judah and Jerusalem, [2] I will gather all nations and bring them down to the Valley of Jehoshaphat. There I will enter into judgment against them concerning my inheritance, my people Israel, for **they scattered my people among the nations and *divided up my land*.**" (Joel 3:1-2)

The prophet Joel wrote almost exclusively about the last days. He noted that God would bring His people back to their Promised Land. He also said that the Gentile nations would divide up that land. This has been a top priority for the United Nations since Israel's statehood (i.e., since May 1948). After their victory in the Six-Day War in 1967, Israel assumed control over additional land. This new territory included the capital city, Jerusalem. Instead of defeating the Jewish state, Jordan, Egypt, and Syria were handed a resounding defeat. These countries had been the aggressors, but Israel, with much help from God, turned them away. However, since that time, this newly acquired land has been a hotly contested geopolitical issue; at times it has led to intermittent skirmishes during the last forty-five years.

Currently, **the West Bank, the Golan Heights, Gaza, and Jerusalem** (e.g., the Temple Mount is under Islamic Waqf control) **have been divided up between the Jewish and Palestinian people**. Israel lays claim to this land since their victory in the Six-Day War. The Palestinians counter that it is their land regardless of the result of any war. The United Nations wants Israel to give up even more land. Their hope is that by giving up more land, peace will follow. Apparently, it is not enough that Israel has to face daily missile attacks originating from Gaza – which began almost immediately after they relinquished that portion of land for "peace." Virtually all foreign nations also want Israel to divide up Jerusalem as well.

Hopefully, Israel will have learned their lesson after what has happened due to their ceding of Gaza to the Palestinians. There has never been any "land for peace" offer that has brought any lasting peace for Israel. Usually, this proposed peace has not even lasted for a matter of weeks. As the saying goes, "Fool me once, shame on you... fool me twice, shame on me."

So we see that the Bible prophesied the situation now experienced by Israel. Their land will continue to be a hotly contested possession until the coming of the Messiah. In fact, in the not too distant future, this current bickering interspersed with relatively small battles will be replaced by an all-out war.

10. Israel Will Deny the True Messiah Until the Time of the Gentiles is Completed:

Although it is true that God has brought His chosen people back into the land of Israel and has granted them all of the blessings that will be discussed in the next chapter and many more, the Bible says that the nation of Israel will still not recognize Jesus as Messiah until the Church Age is over. This will not occur until after the Rapture. Of course, there will always be a remnant that understands and accepts the truth, but God will not turn the nation, as a whole, towards the truth of His Son until the time of the Tribulation.

It is common knowledge that the vast majority of Jews do not believe in Jesus as their Messiah, let alone as the Son of God, at this time. The Bible states that God will lead them back into the truth during and because of the events of the Tribulation. Of course, this will be after the completion of the time of the Gentiles and the Church Age in which we currently live. Jesus, Himself, told the Jews of His time that they would not see Him again until they, as a nation, would be willing to say, "Blessed is He who comes in the name of the Lord."

> "Look, your house is left to you desolate. I tell you, you will not see me again until you say, 'Blessed is he who comes in the name of the Lord.'" (Luke 13:35)

> I do not want you to be ignorant of this mystery, brothers, so that you may not be conceited: **Israel has experienced a hardening in part until the full number of the Gentiles has come in.** 26 And so all Israel will be saved, as it is written: **"The deliverer will come from Zion; he will turn godlessness away from Jacob."** (Isaiah 59:20) (Romans 11:25-26)

The apostle Paul wrote in his epistle to the Romans that one day the nation of Israel will finally recognize the truth of the gospel message. This will occur during the seven year Tribulation just prior to the Second Coming of Jesus. At that time, the vast majority of the Jews will turn to Jesus as their Savior and Lord.

11. The Returning Jews Will Have No King Until Jesus Reigns Over His Millennial Kingdom:

> For the Israelites will live many days without king or prince, **without sacrifice or sacred stones, without ephod or idol.** 5 Afterward the Israelites will return and seek the LORD their God **and David their king.** They will come trembling to the Lord and to His blessings in the last days. (Hosea 3:4-5)

As with all other Bible prophecies, undoubtedly this one is also true. Not since the last king of Judah, Zedekiah, was murdered by the Babylonians has either Judah or Israel been ruled by a king or prince. This was over 2,500 years ago. Amazingly, not only is Israel no longer a theocracy, but today the Jewish state is governed by a democracy comprised of approximately thirty political parties. There are no plans to change this form of government. In fact, this democratic rule will not change until Jesus returns and sets up His Millennial Kingdom on earth. As the verse from Hosea suggests, when the Jews return and seek their Lord God, they will regain both their God and their King. As the last verse says, this will occur "in the last days."

12. The Eastern Gate Will Remain Closed Until the Coming of the Messiah:

> **Then the man brought me back to the** outer gate of the sanctuary, the one facing east, **and it was shut.** ² The LORD said to me, "This gate is to remain shut. **It must not be opened; no one may enter through it. It is to remain shut because the Lord, the God of Israel, has entered through it.** ³ The prince himself is the only one who may sit inside the gateway to eat in the presence of the LORD. **He is to enter by way of the portico of the gateway and go out the same way."** (Ezek 44:1-3)

When Jesus entered into Jerusalem from the Mount of Olives, He, almost assuredly, walked through the Eastern Gate. In A.D. 70, the Roman army totally destroyed the Temple and much of the city. This gate was destroyed at that time. Most historians believe that the gate was rebuilt over the remnants of the earlier one in approximately A.D. 520. About one thousand years later (A.D. 1530), the Ottoman Turks sealed the gate shut to prevent the future prophesied entrance of the Messiah. Even a cemetery was placed in front of this sealed gate for the same purpose... to keep the Messiah from passing through the gate. It is the only one of the eleven gates to the city that has been sealed. Although the Muslim leader, Suleiman, ordered the gate sealed in an attempt to prevent the fulfillment of prophecy, he instead, allowed for its fulfillment.

Ezekiel wrote that the Eastern Gate of the Temple would remain closed until the Messiah returns. At Christ's Second Coming, he will enter Jerusalem through the now sealed Eastern Gate. As one would expect, today, as predicted, the Eastern Gate remains sealed. Interestingly, there have been attempts to foil this prophecy in the past. All have been intriguingly impressive failures:

- On December 9, 1917, the Arab leader of Jerusalem, the Grand Mufti, ordered his workmen to open the Eastern Gate. British General Allenby was advancing with his Expeditionary Army as they fought against the Ottoman Empire. The Grand Mufti had closed the other gates for protection, but still needed access through this Eastern Gate. The story goes that as the workmen picked up their sledgehammers to begin the task of opening the sealed gate, Allenby's airplane flew overhead, dropping leaflets telling the Arabs to flee for their lives. They took his sage advice, dropped their sledgehammers and fled the city. The gate remained closed.

- There was at least one additional serious attempt to open this famous gate. In 1967, King Hussein of Jordan decided to build a hotel for Arab pilgrims immediately adjacent to one section of the Western Wall. Presumably, this would have resulted in the closing of the Western Wall for Jewish worship forever. Hussein already had forbidden the Jews from worshipping at their sacred site in 1948. Along with this hotel, the Jordan king decided to open the Eastern Gate in order to allow for easy access to the El Aksa Mosque built on the Temple Mount. As should not be surprising to those who study Bible prophecy, these plans never materialized. At the same time that plans for beginning construction were being finalized, Arabs prepared to attack the Jewish state of Israel. However, in the famous Six-Day War of June, 1967, Israel crushed their attackers. The Muslims who were preparing to open the Eastern Gate, once again abandoned their air hammers as Israeli aircraft flew menacingly overhead. The Arabs never again attempted to open this gate as the Jews recaptured Jerusalem in that very war. Today, the Eastern Gate remains sealed and will remain sealed until the day the Messiah walks through it.

One day, the Messiah will land on the Mount of Olives with all His saints and will walk down to and right through the Eastern Gate and into the Temple. What will happen with the adjoining cemetery is unknown. Maybe it will be removed via the earthquake that will accompany the return of Jesus. In any case, the Eastern Gate will remain closed until the Messiah returns.

> Then the man brought me to the gate facing east, ² and I saw the glory of the God of Israel coming from the east. His voice was like the roar of rushing waters, and the land was radiant with his glory. ³ The vision I saw was like the vision I had seen when he came to destroy the city and like the visions I had seen by the Kebar River, and I fell facedown. ⁴ The glory of **the Lord entered the temple through the gate facing east**. ⁵ Then the Spirit lifted me up and brought me into the inner court, and the glory of the LORD filled the temple. (Ezek 43:1-5)

Figure 1: The Eastern Gate – closed until the return of the Messiah

Figure 2: Model of the Jewish Temple and surrounding Jerusalem

Chapter 3

God Will Bless the Land of Israel

ONCE THE JEWS returned to their homeland, God promised that He would begin the process of blessing their land. This promise can be seen in the writings of the Old Testament prophets. Moses, Ezekiel, Isaiah, Amos, and Joel spoke of some of these latter day blessings of the land.

Although much of Palestine recently existed primarily as a desert landscape, God said in the end times that He would provide adequate water to support bountiful growth. God has honored His promise, as always. Forests have recently flourished; vegetables and flowers now grow in abundance, and wineries are numerous and prosperous. The exciting story of God's transformation of the land is detailed in the chapter below. Not only has God transformed the land above ground, He has arranged for those in Israel to recognize and discover the vast resources of energy that lie beneath the ground and sea. All of these blessings have brought great riches to the Jews and their nation of Israel. There is still more to come.

13. **God Will Bless the Land of Israel with Rain and Other Sources of Water in the Latter Days:**

> "I will make rivers flow on barren heights, and springs within the valleys. **I will turn the desert into pools of**

water, and the parched ground into springs. ¹⁹ I will put in the desert the cedar and the acacia, the myrtle and the olive. **I will set pines in the wasteland, the fir and the cypress together,** ²⁰ **so that people may see and know, may consider and understand, that the hand of the Lord has done this, that the Holy One of Israel has created it."** (Isaiah 41:18-20)

Be glad, O people of Zion, rejoice in the LORD your God, for he has given you the autumn rains in righteousness. **He sends you abundant showers**, both autumn and spring rains, as before. (Joel 2:23)

In the verses above, the prophets Isaiah and Joel are writing of the latter days. God reveals that He will bless the land of Israel with rain and will change the topography of Israel in these end times. The desert plains and the wilderness will no longer be arid. Instead, in some fashion, God states that water will appear once again as in Old Testament days. Not only that, but with water now available on the once arid land of Israel, trees will come back onto the land, and, as we shall see below, fruit, vegetables, and grapes will now grow in abundance. It is interesting to note from the verses in Isaiah above, God is doing all of this, in part, so that the world will know what "the hand of the Lord has done." In fact, the vast majority of the signs that will be presented in this section are given by God so that those who are watching expectantly will understand that the coming of the Lord is growing near.

When the displaced Jews began their return in earnest in the last half of the twentieth century, many brilliant agricultural engineers worked hard to develop the most sophisticated irrigation systems in the entire world. Drip-irrigation techniques have enabled them to use virtually every drop of water available. The outstanding fertilizer product from the Dead Sea has also allowed the Israeli farmer to once again turn that land into lush gardens.

Over 240 million trees were planted in Israel during the twentieth century. Israel is the only nation on earth that ended that century with more trees than it began. An active effort by the people in Israel and many people around the world who support them have teamed up to reforest much of that land. Now there are scores of forested acres around that country. Dozens of types of trees now grow, including, the olive, almond, fig, date palm, pistachio, acacia, oak, pine and many more. It is an impressive sight to see the satellite image of Israel as compared to the surrounding Arab countries. Israel is virtually completely green while their counterparts to the east and south appear brown from the vantage point of space.[9]

Although it is still true that Israel could use more rainfall, this past century has noted a significant increase compared to the previous several centuries. Grant Jeffrey wrote that "the rainfall in Palestine has increased dramatically by over ten percent every single decade during the last century because the returning Jewish exiles planted more than 200 million trees, transforming the complete environment of the Promised Land."[10] Others note that the rainfall has increased since 1900, but not quite as much as quoted by Jeffrey. In any case, due to the increased forestation, the outstanding irrigation advancements, and the increased rainfall, Israel is fast growing into the beautiful and lush nation promised by God so many centuries ago. One might well assume from this that the end-times promised appearance of Jesus is soon to come.

14. Israel Shall Blossom and Bud, and Fill the Face of the World with Fruit (Isaiah 27:6):

In the verse above, Isaiah tells of God's blessing on the land of Israel in the end times. However, in the twenty-ninth chapter of Deuteronomy, the prophet Moses tells of the many centuries that God's judgment will have turned the land of Israel into a virtual desert leading up to their eventual time of blessing. During that time of judgment, there will be no water to speak of and no agriculture.

> The whole land will be a burning waste of salt and sulfur-- nothing planted, nothing sprouting, no vegetation growing on it. .... [24] All the nations will ask: "**Why has the Lord done this to this land?** Why this fierce, burning anger?" [25] And the answer will be: "**It is because this people abandoned the covenant of the Lord, the God of their fathers.**" (Deut 29:23-25)

After the Romans brutally defeated the Jews in the war of A.D. 70, the army of Rome stripped the land of much of its trees and orchards. The Promised Land would be abandoned and it would become primarily a desert wasteland. It would continue in this pitiable condition for multiple centuries. Mark Twain wrote of his trip to Israel in his book, *Innocents Abroad* in the late nineteenth century, "There is no timber of any consequence. There was hardly a tree or shrub anywhere. Even the olive and the cactus, those fast friends of a worthless soul, had almost deserted the country. ... A desolation is here that not even imagination can grace with the pomp of life and action. ... Jerusalem is mournful and dreary and lifeless. I would not desire to live here. ... It is truly monotonous and uninviting and there is no sufficient reason for describing it as otherwise. Of all the lands there are for dismal scenery, I think Palestine must be the prince. The hills are barren, they are dull of color, they are unpicturesque in shape. The valleys are unsightly deserts, fringed with a feeble vegetation that has an expression about it of being sorrowful and despondent. It is a hopeless, dreary, heart-broken land. Palestine sits in sackcloth and ashes. Over it broods the spell of a curse that has withered its fields and fettered its energies."[11]

However, all of that has changed miraculously! The verse that introduced this sign was a prophecy given to Isaiah over 2,600 years ago. **"Israel shall blossom and bud, and fill the face of the world with fruit"** (Isaiah 27:6).

As was previously discussed, Israel has in this last century been blessed with more rainfall and has developed state-of-the-art irrigation techniques that are the envy of the world. Not only has Israel added a quarter million trees, but God has intervened to turn this land into a place of beauty in many other areas as noted below.

> **"In the latter years you will come into the land** of those brought back from the sword and gathered from many people on the mountains of Israel, **which had long been desolate; they were brought out of the nations."** (Ezek 38:8, NKJV)

> "I will bring back my exiled people Israel; they will rebuild the ruined cities and live in them. **They will plant vineyards and drink their wine; they will make gardens and eat their fruit.** ¹⁵ I will plant Israel in their own land, never again to be uprooted."** (Amos 9:14-15)

> **"But you, O mountains of Israel, will produce branches and fruit for my people Israel, for they will soon come home.** ⁹ I am concerned for you and will look on you with favor; you will be plowed and sown." (Ezek 36:8-9)

> "The desolate land will be cultivated instead of lying desolate in the sight of all who pass through it. ³⁵ They will say, **'This land that was laid waste has become like the garden of Eden**; the cities that were lying in ruins, desolate and destroyed, are now fortified and inhabited.' ³⁶ Then the nations around you that remain will know that I the LORD have rebuilt what was destroyed and have replanted what was desolate. I the LORD have spoken, and I will do it." (Ezek 36:34-36)

Since Israel gained its independence in 1948, they have tripled the area of land suitable for cultivation. Now there are approximately 1.2 million arable acres of land. Even more impressive, their production has increased 16-fold since those early years. In fact, they have become a major exporter of many agricultural products.[12]

Israel is currently able to produce 95% of its own food requirements and has become a major exporter of vegetables, fruits, and flowers to the rest of the world. Flowers (25%), vegetables and field crops (wheat and corn and sorghum – 45%), and fruit (25% including 10% citrus) comprise most of this list. They export more than forty fruits and a wide variety of vegetables. Cotton is also a major exported crop – nearly $125 million worth per year. Israel is one of the world's largest flower producers and exporters, even exporting tulips to Amsterdam! The scientists in Israel have made great strides and are world leaders in research and development in modern agricultural techniques, soil enhancers, fertilizers, and irrigation methods. Because of the greater quantity of rain and the excellent irrigation methods, the Jewish farmer can now plant more than one crop per year. This was not possible until the latter portion of this past century.[13]

This is another of the signs that God specifically notes should cause other nations and people to pause and recognize His providential power working in the world. He spoke through Ezekiel and said, "Then the nations around you that remain will know that I the LORD have rebuilt what was destroyed and have replanted what was desolate" (Ezek 36:36).

15. Israel Will Once Again, in the End Times, Produce Sweet Wine in Abundance:

> "Then you will know that I, the LORD your God, dwell in Zion, my holy hill. Jerusalem will be holy; never again will foreigners invade her. [18] **In that day the mountains will**

45

> **drip new wine**, and the hills will flow with milk; all the ravines of Judah will run with water." (Joel 3:17-18)
>
> **"The days are coming,"** declares the LORD, "when the reaper will be overtaken by the plowman and the planter by the one treading grapes. **New wine will drip from the mountains and flow from all the hills.**[14] I will bring back my exiled people Israel; they will rebuild the ruined cities and live in them. **They will plant vineyards and drink their wine; they will make gardens and eat their fruit.**[15] **I will plant Israel in their own land, never again to be uprooted from the land I have given them,"** says the LORD your God. (Amos 9:13-15)

Since coming home to Israel in 1948, the Jewish people have made extraordinary progress in the development of their land. Remember, the land in that area was mostly desert in the hundreds of years before God brought His people back to the land promised to Abraham.

Now, Israeli wine is produced by hundreds of wineries. A few of the larger companies produce over ten million bottles per year. In 2010, Israeli wine exports amounted to $30 million produced by 150 wineries.

"The modern Israeli wine industry was founded by Baron Edmond James de Rothschild, owner of the Bordeaux estate Château Lafite-Rothschild. Today, Israeli winemaking takes place in five vine growing regions: Galilee (including the Golan Heights); the Judean Hills, surrounding the city of Jerusalem; Shimshon (Samson), located between the Judean Hills and the Coastal Plain; the Negev, a semi-arid desert region, where drip irrigation has made grape growing possible; and the Sharon plain near the Mediterranean coast and just south of Haifa, which is the largest grape growing area in Israel. In 2007, Robert Parker's The Wine Advocate awarded fourteen Israeli wines its highest wine rating of 'outstanding.'"[14]

Israel has emerged as an excellent producer of wine in the Mediterranean region. It exports much of what it produces, more to the United States than to any other country. Along with the land being very suitable for the growing of excellent grapes, Israel is a world leader in the technological aspects of wine production. Merlot, Cabernet Sauvignon, and Chardonnay are three of the more popular types of wine coming from Israel. There is no doubt that the prophets Joel and Amos were correct when they made their end-times prophecies some 2,500 years ago. As Amos said, "New wine will drip from the mountains and flow from all the hills." Also note again that the prophet said once Israel is re-established in their land, they will never again be uprooted.

16. Israel Will Become a Nation with Many Natural Resources in the Latter Days:

The coming war prophesied in Ezekiel will bring Russia, Iran, and many Arab nations against Israel. This war will be discussed in some detail later on in this book. It is easy to understand why all of these nations will want to come against Israel, except for possibly Russia. Every one of the nations mentioned by Ezekiel has an inherent and long-standing hatred for the Jews... and they want to see them eliminated. However, Russia will want something more. Many prophecy scholars believe that they will be coming to defeat Israel because they will want to receive a bounty. Russia will want the valuable resources that will be available in Israel during the end times. In fact, this is what Ezekiel says concerning Magog, the nation now known as Russia...

> The word of the LORD came to me:[2] "Son of man, set your face against Gog, of the land of **Magog**, the chief prince of Meshech and Tubal; prophesy against him[3] and say: 'This is what the Sovereign LORD says: **I am against you, O Gog [the leader of Russia], chief prince of Meshech and**

> **Tubal.⁴ I will turn you around, put hooks in your jaws
> and bring you out with your whole army [God will be
> behind Russia's attack against Israel in the end time]**--
> your horses, your horsemen fully armed, and a great horde
> with large and small shields, all of them brandishing their
> swords'" … "This is what the Sovereign LORD says: **On
> that day thoughts will come into your mind and you will
> devise an evil scheme.¹¹ You will say, 'I will invade a land
> of unwalled villages [Israel]**; I will attack a peaceful and
> unsuspecting people--all of them living without walls
> and without gates and bars.¹² **I will plunder and loot and
> turn my hand against the resettled ruins and the people
> gathered from the nations, rich in livestock and goods,**
> living at the center of the land.'" (Ezek 38:3-4,10-12)

It is definitely true that Israel has become a land rich in agricultural products in these last sixty years. Israel, as we have seen, is doing extremely well in many areas of production. However, it is true that most countries are still typically interested in acquiring two items more than any others when it comes to the natural resources of other countries; that is, energy products (e.g., oil and gas) and minerals. That begs the question… how is Israel doing with respect to these items? The answer will surprise many.

Everyone knows that the Arab countries currently have a monopoly on oil. The top five countries in oil production are Saudi Arabia, Iran, Iraq, Kuwait and United Arab Emirates. The United States ranks eleventh. What about Israel? Until recently, their energy production has been very low.

However, there are people who have actually taken the Old Testament to heart and formed companies to search for oil and natural gas based on what is written in these Scriptures. They have done this because the Bible strongly suggests that much natural bounty from the earth and sea will be discovered in and around Israel as the world approaches the end times.

Beginning in the 1990s, there have been companies formed to search for oil and natural gas in Israel and the adjoining Mediterranean Sea. Joel Rosenberg, a writer of best-selling books on eschatology, wondered about just this topic while writing his recent book, *Epicenter.* He also happens to be an insider with respect to Israel as he used to work for their current Prime Minister, Benjamin Netanyahu. Joel devoted an entire chapter of his book to show how recent discoveries of both oil and natural gas have excited many people. Many believe there will be even greater discoveries in the near future.

> And of Joseph he said: "Blessed of the LORD is his land, With the precious things of heaven, with the dew, and **the deep lying beneath,**[14] With **the precious fruits of the sun,** With the precious produce of the months,[15] **With the best things of the ancient mountains, With the precious things of the everlasting hills,**[16] **With the precious things of the earth and its fullness.**" (Deut 33:13-16, NKJV)

Many scholars, including a Russian Jewish geophysicist and oil man named Tovia Luskin, believe verses such as the one noted above point to oil and/or natural gas lying beneath the surface in the land God gave to Israel. A Christian entrepreneur, John Brown, came to the same conclusion through his study of the Old Testament Scriptures. Both men now have companies searching Israel for these products. Gene Soltero, an MIT trained petroleum engineer, is another oil man now doing the same thing. He is the CEO of Zion Oil, the company founded by John Brown. These people, and many others, are putting their money and time where their beliefs lie...[15]

Rosenberg listed some of the Bible verses that have excited these oil men:

1. Because of your father's God, who helps you, because of the Almighty, who blesses you with blessings of the

heavens above, **blessings of the deep that lies below...**
(Genesis 49:25)

2. Deuteronomy 33:13-16 (see above)
3. They will **feast on the abundance of the seas, on the treasures hidden in the sand.** (Deuteronomy 33:19)
4. Most blessed of sons is Asher; let him be favored by his brothers, and **let him bathe his feet in oil.** (Deuteronomy 33:24)
5. The Lord alone led him... He nourished him with **honey from the rock, and with oil from the flinty crag [rock].** (Deuteronomy 32:12-13)
6. **I will give you the treasures of darkness, riches stored in secret places,** so that you may know that I am the Lord, the God of Israel, who summons you by name. (Isaiah 45:3)

Since all of these Bible-believing oil entrepreneurs have begun to search for oil and natural gas in Israel, some really positive results have begun to materialize. Incredible quantities of natural gas, oil and shale have been discovered within just the last several years.

"Off the coast of Israel in the waters of the Mediterranean Sea, explorers have found what is being called the largest offshore gas reserve in the world and the biggest find in a decade."[16] There have been several discoveries of offshore natural gas fields very recently. Noble Energy has two recent finds that they have named the Tamar and Leviathan Gas Fields. Together they will combine to yield twenty-five trillion cubic feet of gas. This is double the natural gas available to Britain in the North Sea. The Tamar Field alone should be able to provide all of Israel's gas needs for at least twenty years. The larger field, Leviathan, will be used for exporting energy for decades to come. In fact, recently Israel has been talking with Greece about not only becoming one of the many nations to which it will export their new found energy products, but also to partner to build the necessary pipe lines for exporting their gas and oil to other countries.[17] An even more massive deposit, estimated at 122 trillion cubic feet of natural gas, has been found in an area that is mapped out by the triangle extending from the Gaza Strip to Cypress to Lebanon. This is now known as the Levant Basin Province. "Some economists estimate that the natural gas will add $300 billion to the Israeli economy over time, which is 150% of the country's entire GDP."[18] Many have called this the largest offshore gas reserve in the entire world. Of course, this will likely mean that Israel will soon become a major player in the energy field worldwide – certainly by the end of this decade, if not sooner. The rest of the world is taking notice. A recent Wall Street Journal headline reported… "BIG GAS FIND SPARKS A FRENZY IN ISRAEL."[19]

In addition to these enormous natural gas discoveries, it is also reported that more than four billion barrels of crude oil lie beneath these gas fields. This is more than 20% of the entire United States total oil reserves.[20] New discoveries of these important energy sources are being made on a regular basis. For example, in March 2012, Israel's Modlin Energy Partnership discovered two new oil fields off the coast of Tel Aviv. These fields were named Gabriella and Yitzhak. Surveys suggest that they will eventually yield over 230 million barrels of oil and 1.8 trillion cubic feet of natural gas.[21]

The energy finds do not stop with natural gas and oil. "In addition to natural gas, it appears the Jewish state is also rich in oil shale – a fine-grained rock which can be used to produce oil through a special process. Harold Vinegar, chief scientist with Israel Energy Initiatives, says the amount of oil shale buried here might equal the oil reserves of Saudi Arabia. "We think it's conservatively estimated at about 250 billion barrels of oil contained in the Israeli oil shale – probably the second or third largest deposit in the whole world," Vinegar said. "And it has a tremendous potential to make an oil industry here. Experts say there's enough oil shale to produce at least 50,000 barrels of oil a day – enough to meet Israel's military and civil aviation needs for 25 years."[22]

All of these energy sources will soon be available for use. It will not be long before Israel is thought of in the same way as their Arab Middle Eastern neighbors, those that constitute OPEC. Golda Meir used to lament about the course that Moses took after he led the Israelites out of Egypt and across the Red Sea, "He dragged us forty years through the desert to bring us to the one place in the Middle East that has no oil." As it turns out, it has become apparent that Ms. Meir was in error when she questioned God's wisdom in directing the Israelites to the Promised Land.

Not only does Israel show evidence of soon being a major player in the energy field, they also are producing in several other areas. They have become a big producer in technology. Bill Gates (the Microsoft billionaire) has been quoted as saying that "Israel is like part of Silicon Valley." Wall Street tycoon, Warren Buffet, recently invested four billion to purchase 80% of an Israeli *metal working company*. This was the largest corporate deal in Israel's history. Israel is also a leader in *microchip production, industrial oils, diamonds, fertilizers, many minerals*, etc. The Dead Sea is a source of great wealth to Israel. *Magnesium chloride, sodium chloride, calcium chloride, potassium chloride and magnesium bromide* are all available in great quantities from this sea... **estimates of their worth range into the trillions of dollars.** Israel is ranked far ahead of Syria, Egypt, Jordan, and Lebanon in gross domestic product. Benjamin Netanyahu recently stated, **"In ten years, Israel could be one of the ten richest countries in the world."** With their recent energy discoveries, this time estimate may well be cut in half.[23]

It is therefore no wonder that one day soon Russia will join forces with Iran and other Arab states in an attempt to take over the land of Israel. However, God will not allow Israel to be defeated.

Figure 3: Springtime in Israel – Fields of Flowers

Figure 4: Israeli Vineyard

Chapter 4

THE THIRD TEMPLE WILL STAND DURING THE TRIBULATION

THE BIBLE LEAVES no doubt that the Third Temple will be standing by the midpoint of the seven year Tribulation. Many Bible verses make this clear and will be quoted in the paragraphs below. Given that it will take at least a couple of years to build this great Temple, it only seems reasonable that a great deal of Temple preparation must be accomplished prior to the onset of this period. Therefore, if the premise of this book is correct and the Rapture is soon to occur, much work regarding the building and furnishing of this Tribulation Temple should already have taken place. As will be shown in the signs listed below, every necessary item is completely in place at this time to enable builders to commence building right now. They only await the word to lay that first foundation stone. Although it may happen earlier, most prophecy scholars believe that the Temple will be completed during the first couple of years of the Tribulation. Much has already been accomplished in the preparations for the building of the Tribulation Temple.

17. The Sanhedrin Has Been Re-established After Over 1,500 Years:

On October 13, 2004, seventy-one rabbis were ordained into the newly formed Sanhedrin. This was quite a momentous occasion as this august ruling body had not been in existence for over 1,500 years. The original Sanhedrin court met for the first time when Moses selected seventy leaders to help him judge the people after they left Egypt...

> The LORD said to Moses: "**Bring me seventy of Israel's elders** who are known to you as leaders and officials among the people. Have them come to the Tent of Meeting, that they may stand there with you.[17] I will come down and speak with you there, and I will take of the Spirit that is on you and put the Spirit on them. **They will help you carry the burden of the people** so that you will not have to carry it alone." (Num 11:16-17)

Ezra reinstituted this ruling body after the Jews returned from Babylon. It continued until A.D. 425 when it met for the last time in Tiberias. The Roman Emperor, Theodosius, originally ordered their disbandment in the latter part of the fourth century. His grandson, Theodosius II, removed all vestiges of this court in the year A.D. 425. Since that time, Israel and the Jewish people have been without this court to rule on important religious issues. However, since early 2005, the new Sanhedrin has met regularly to discuss things such as the building of the Third Temple, the selection and training of Levitical priests for future positions in the Temple, and many other important religious topics. In recent years, they have worked to hire architects to develop plans for the Third Temple and raise money for all necessary future religious projects. The most important of these projects is the building of the Temple and acquiring all of its associated furniture and utensils.

The return of the Sanhedrin is very important in regards to the return of Jesus. **For the Temple to be rebuilt, and the many prophecies to be fulfilled related to this, the Sanhedrin must be in their proper spiritual and political leadership position.** Now this has been accomplished. The most important decisions concerning the Temple will be made by this body of rabbis. For decades, a major stumbling block to the rebuilding was the fact that one of the most holy structures in Islam, the Dome of the Rock, already stood on the Temple Mount. It did not make any reasonable political sense to consider removing this structure in order to build the Jewish Temple. However, recent studies have suggested, interestingly, that the Temple might be able to be built without removing the Muslim's Dome of the Rock. As it turns out, there is evidence that has convinced several prophecy scholars that the Dome of the Rock does not occupy the same area where the Second Temple once stood.[24] Therefore, if true, the newly rebuilt Third Temple would occupy an adjacent area on the Temple Mount. The final decision concerning this will be made by the new Sanhedrin ruling body after careful study and consideration of the all of the archaeological and historical records. This is just one example of the type of decision that the Sanhedrin are now able to make that will affect future Jewish religious life in Israel.

18. The Third Temple Will Exist During the Tribulation:

Plans for the Third Temple are well underway and a great amount of effort is being expended in preparation for the rebuilding of the Temple of God. It is abundantly clear through the reading of the Scriptures that the Temple will be standing and in use during the Tribulation. Note just a few of these verses...

> **"Go and measure the temple of God and the altar,** and count the worshipers there.[2] But exclude the outer court; do not measure it, because it has been given to

the Gentiles. They will trample on the holy city for 42 months." (Rev 11:1-2)

"In that day I will restore David's fallen tent, I will repair its broken places, restore its ruins." (Amos 9:11)

"His armed forces will rise up to desecrate the temple fortress and **will abolish the daily sacrifice.** Then they will set up the abomination that causes desolation." (Dan 11:31)

Don't let anyone deceive you in any way, for **that day will not come until the rebellion occurs and the man of lawlessness is revealed, the man doomed to destruction.**[4] He will oppose and will exalt himself over everything that is called God or is worshiped, so that **he sets himself up in God's temple, proclaiming himself to be God.** (2 Thess 2:3-4)

There is absolutely no doubt that there will be a Third Temple in Jerusalem during the Tribulation period that follows the Rapture. There are many verses that support this fact. For example, the books of Daniel and The Revelation note that halfway through the Tribulation, the Temple of God will be desecrated by the Antichrist. Obviously, the Temple must be in place for this to occur. That being true, and knowing that the Tribulation most probably begins soon after the Rapture, it is likely that significant plans related to the rebuilding of the Temple would already be underway before Jesus comes for His saints in the air (i.e., the Rapture). As it turns out, the Israelis' have spent a great amount of time and money preparing to build their next Temple and return to proper Temple worship as directed in their Scriptures.

For at least twenty years, the Temple Institute has put forth much effort in planning for the building of the next Temple. Recent reports suggest that the plans are complete. In fact, the architectural plans for the Temple can be studied over the Internet. In an Internet article entitled, "The Greatest Progress Toward the Rebuilding of the Holy Temple," the complete blueprints for the Chamber of Hewn Stone: the Seat of the Great Sanhedrin are available for all interested to review.[25] Even the cornerstones for the Temple have been cut and consecrated and are ready for placement.

All that awaits is the proper political situation to allow for the groundbreaking to erect what will become the Third Temple, the Tribulation Temple. Most prophecy scholars believe that this situation will come about very soon after the Antichrist comes onto the world scene and brokers a landmark peace treaty between Israel and her enemies. While basking in his victory, and with the knowledge that he will one day take over the use of the Temple himself, he will allow the Jews to build their Temple. However, this peace will be a false peace, soon to come crashing down when the Antichrist desecrates the Temple just 3 ½ years later.

19. Sacred Temple Vessels:

When the Jews once again are given the opportunity to use their Temple they will have all of the necessary Temple equipment, clothing, utensils and vessels described in the Old Testament. Intriguingly, artisans have been excitedly at work in fashioning all of these needed items for many years. The people of the Temple Institute have prepared well over a hundred sacred worship objects described in the Torah. These articles even include the linen garments for the Levite priests. Some of these items are quite expensive. For example, a menorah completed over a decade ago and just waiting for use in the Temple, cost over $400,000 to complete. It consists of over ninety-two pounds of pure gold. In 2007, the Temple Institute announced the completion of the golden crown (i.e., head plate) for the High Priest. This is called the tzitz. It took one year to make and is made of pure gold. Virtually everything is ready and waiting for service in the Third Temple. In fact, the Temple Institute's leader, Rabbi Chaim Richman, has stated that *everything* that is required to resume divine worship services and to build the Temple is currently available.

20. Levitical Priesthood:

One other interesting aspect of the work of the Temple Institute is their recruiting and training of men for the priesthood. Since there is going to be a Jewish Temple on the Temple Mount soon after the onset of the Tribulation, there must be a large number of well-trained priests to carry out the many duties required to run this Temple properly. To recruit and train these priests will take a lot of time. Of course, these men must also come from the tribe of Levi.

As it turns out, orthodox Jewish Bible colleges (yeshivas) have already trained over five hundred young men for this important position. It is interesting to note that genetic markings have been used to determine those eligible to become priests of the coming Temple. A registry is now kept of all known men of the proper lineage.

All of the necessary training, including the preparation for the playing of musical instruments, has been completed. These priests are only waiting for the right moment of opportunity and now stand ready to serve their God.

While they wait, they will soon have the opportunity to perform their duties in a full scale model of the Third Temple that is being built in Mitzpe Yericho, not very far from Jerusalem. The purpose of this facility will be to give hands-on training to Cohanim (i.e., a Jew who is a descendent of Aaron) and other Levitical priests who will one day assume the important duties of a Temple priest. This is a position of great responsibility and must be taken very seriously.

21. Oil of Anointing:

The special oil required for Temple worship services was prepared by the priests using five specific ingredients. This oil was used to anoint the Temple, the Ark of the Covenant, and the High Priest. It will be needed for proper Temple worship in the future Temple.

> **"Make these into a sacred anointing oil**, a fragrant blend, the work of a perfumer. It will be the sacred anointing oil.²⁶ Then **use it to anoint the Tent of Meeting**, the ark of the Testimony,²⁷ **the table and all its articles, the lampstand and its accessories, the altar of incense,** ²⁸ **the altar of burnt offering and all its utensils, and the basin with its stand.**²⁹ You shall consecrate them so they will be most holy, and whatever touches them will be holy."³⁰ **"Anoint Aaron and his sons and consecrate them so they may serve me as priests.**³¹ Say to the Israelites, **'This is to be my sacred anointing oil for the generations to come.'"** (Ex 30:25-31)

This would appear to present a problem. Where would one find this oil so many years after Jerusalem and the Temple were razed to the ground? One of the ingredients, from a rare plant called "sweet cinnamon" was apparently lost forever some two thousand years ago. Substitutions would not do. Unfortunately, Roman soldiers burned down the only two groves in Israel where this plant was known to grow in A.D. 70. No one knows where, or if, it is still available today.²⁶ Jewish scholars throughout history taught that the lack of the special and necessary "oil of anointing" was going to make reinstituting Temple worship impossible. The priests would not be able to anoint the Temple with the proper oil as commanded by God. Not only that, but Daniel prophesied that the Messiah would be anointed with the oil upon His return. "Seventy 'sevens' are decreed for your people and your holy city to finish transgression, to put an end to sin, to atone for wickedness, to bring in everlasting righteousness, to seal up vision and prophecy and **to anoint the most holy**" (Dan 9:24). Well, God could certainly take care of this problem. In fact, it appears that He did.

In 1952, a now famous copper scroll was found in "Cave 8" at Qumran (one of the Dead Sea caves) during an archaeological excavation. This scroll revealed information that then led other archaeologists to another cave, Cave 811, where a clay vessel containing a solidified gelatinous substance was discovered. It was buried three feet deep and wrapped in palm leaves. The hope was that this gel was the ancient "oil of anointing." The actual oil prescribed by God had five specific ingredients as noted in Exodus 30:23-26. These were myrrh, sweet cinnamon, sweet calamus, cassia, and a hin of olive oil. Incredibly, chemical analysis has shown this clay jar to contain the actual "oil of anointing." This oil is 2,000 years old.[27] Everything is now ready to go, once the future Temple is in place.

> "Then the LORD said to Moses, "Take the following fine spices: 500 shekels of liquid **myrrh**, half as much (that is, 250 shekels) of **fragrant cinnamon**, 250 shekels of **fragrant cane**, 500 shekels of **cassia**--all according to the sanctuary shekel--and **a hin of olive oil**." (Ex 30:22-24)

22. Ark of the Covenant:

> "In those days, when your numbers have increased greatly in the land," declares the LORD, "men will no longer say, **'The ark of the covenant of the Lord.' It will never enter their minds or be remembered; it will not be missed** [nor shall they visit it - NKJV], **nor will another one be made.** [17] At that time they will call Jerusalem the Throne of the LORD, and all nations will gather in Jerusalem to honor the name of the LORD. No longer will they follow the stubbornness of their evil hearts. [18] In those days the

house of Judah will join the house of Israel, and together
they will come from a northern land to the land I gave
your forefathers as an inheritance." (Jer 3:16-18)

The verses written by Jeremiah reveal that after the Jews are
settled in Jerusalem during the Millennial Kingdom, and Jesus
Christ reigns from His throne, the Ark of the Covenant will no
longer be needed. Therefore, it will no longer be something that
any of the people think about or visit any longer. That verse, of
course, suggests that prior to the onset of the Kingdom, the Ark
was something that was on the mind of the people, and was used
in their worship (i.e., they "visited" it). Given that the actual Ark
of the Covenant has not been used for worship in the Temple for
over 2,500 years, it is very logical to conclude that it will be brought
back into service during the Tribulation. It would certainly be odd
if the Temple were rebuilt, the Levitical Priests returned to their
proper duties, all of the Temple services were reinstituted... except
for the most important of all, those services requiring the Ark of
the Covenant. For all of these reasons, it is apparent that the Ark
will be returned in time for use in the Third Temple of God. It is
interesting to review the recent evidence with respect to the current
location of the famous Ark. Grant Jeffrey spent a great deal of time
reviewing this data in his book, *Armageddon: Appointment with
Destiny.*

First of all, it is actually true that the Ark of the Covenant was
pursued by the Axis Powers in the 1930s. Mussolini, in particular,
wanted to find and possess this great Judeo-Christian artifact
because of the powers that it was purported to have. Hitler also was
intrigued by the possibilities that his evil mind was able to conjure
up. The possession of this Ark was the prize goal of the Nazis in
the popular movie, *Raiders of the Lost Ark.* The reason Mussolini
went into Ethiopia is because that was the location that the Ark (or
an exact duplicate) was taken by the son of King Solomon through

the Queen of Sheba. This young man, Prince Menelik I, may have taken the actual Ark there for safekeeping.

Supposedly, Solomon ordered his craftsmen to build an exact replica of the actual Ark so that his beloved son could take it back with him to Ethiopia when he returned there as a young man. Many believe that Menelik, in fact, took the actual Ark in an effort to keep it safe from foreign invaders that he feared would take it from Israel after the death of his father. The unfortunate fact is that Solomon was being adversely influenced late in his life by pagan women. In any case, Menelik did return to Ethiopia with one of the two arks and took many Jews along with him. Of course, these Jews grew greatly in number through the centuries. They are now called the Falasha Jews. These are the Jews who returned in the 1990s as discussed earlier.

Over the years, many people have reported that the Ark is in Ethiopia. Most of these people believe that it ended up in Aksum, a holy city in Ethiopia - in the Church of St. Mary. Grant Jeffrey wrote in great detail about many varied reports over the last eighty years concerning the Ark being safely guarded in Ethiopia. For example, Prince Mengesha Seyoum, the governor-general of Ethiopia, was interviewed on American television in 1990. He stated that the Ark was safely hidden and protected in St Mary's of Zion in Aksum. He even showed a secret underground passage with an elaborate system of tunnels where the Ark has been kept for all these centuries (approximately 3,000 years).[28] This is one of three current popular theories as to the whereabouts of the famous Ark of the Covenant. One other theory follows.

There are many people who believe that the Ark that Menelik took with him was, in fact, a copy. The real Ark was left back in the Temple. Of course, the Temple no longer exists. However, many prophecy scholars say that the Ark was hidden underground in an extremely elaborate and deep tunnel system way back around the time of Solomon. The exact time that the Ark was hidden away is not known. Yet, there are Hebrew priests who have claimed to have actually seen the Ark of the Covenant under the Temple Mount carefully hidden away. On May 15, 1992, on the show "Ancient Secrets of the Bible," Rabbi Yahuda Getz claimed to have seen the Ark under the Temple Mount in one of the tunnel chambers... from about a fifty foot distance. Another Jewish man, Rabbi Shlomo Goren, was with him. They were afraid of violating proper scriptural procedure and did not immediately walk right up to it. This is understandable as the Bible reports that others have dropped dead in their tracks for improper handling of the Ark. Before they had a better opportunity to examine these holy items of God, the Arabs broke through and into the tunnel structure from above and sealed the entire contents from further examination. Apparently, the items that were seen in the underground tunnels at that time will have to wait for another opportunity to be revealed to the world.

There is even one more story concerning the Ark and its current whereabouts. In this report, sources told Grant Jeffrey that an elite team of Israeli Special Forces flew into Ethiopia, carried the Ark out from its location beneath the Church of St. Mary, and then took it back to its current, secure location in Jerusalem. The real Ark, they say, is now back in Jerusalem awaiting the new Temple.

In summary, the real Ark is either in an underground secure tunnel system in Ethiopia, underneath the Temple Mount in one of its many tunnel systems, or nearby the Temple Mount somewhere safe in Jerusalem. Of course, it may even be somewhere else. Time will tell. However, many prophecy scholars do believe that it is in one of the three locations mentioned above. If not, God will reveal its actual location at the proper time.

23. Blue Dye for the Garments of the High Priest:

> "You shall make the robe of the ephod all of blue.
> (Ex 28:31)

64

The high priest wore robes that were dyed with a very special blue dye. More importantly, this blue dye came from a rare source. This dye was known as *tekhelet*. After the destruction of the Second Temple, the source of this dye vanished. Jewish sources wrote that it was going to be impossible to reinstitute proper Temple worship due to this serious problem – God requires that His instructions be followed to the letter and the High Priest's robe must be colored with the appropriate colored dyes from the appropriate source. Of course, this would include the use of this particular blue dye.

Through a careful study of the Torah and the Talmud, it has been determined that this blue dye had to originate from a particular snail and be completely colorfast (i.e., a permanent dye). It also had to be the same color as the dye made from the plant, *Indigofera tinctoria* that was common in the days when Moses wrote the Torah. Today this plant dye is called *kala ilan*.

Rabbinic sources have determined that the appropriate snail was called the *hilazon*. Unfortunately, this is not the name of a particular species, but only a rabbinic name. Someone or some group of marine biologists faced the challenge of determining the particular species of snail, and finding out whether it still existed in the world today. Isaac Herzog, a very bright graduate student who was destined to become a chief rabbi of Israel many years later, accepted this challenge. While writing his doctoral thesis on this topic, he found that the Murex trunculus snail satisfied all of the requirements noted above. He noted that archaeologists had "uncovered large ancient dyeing facilities close to Haifa, and mounds of Murex trunculus broken open, apparently to access their dye."[29] The blue dye is easily extracted from a particular gland on the snail. Herzog was fairly certain that this was the particular snail referenced in the Torah, but was puzzled by the fact that the color he produced from it was more purple than expected. The solution to that problem came almost eighty years later.

In the early 1980s, a Professor from Shenkar College of Engineering and Design, Otto Elsner, made the necessary discovery of how this snail was able to produce the beautiful color blue required by the Torah and Talmud. He noticed that on sunny days, the dye produced by the Murex Trunculus snail always took on a distinctly blue hue. In fact, he realized that by simply exposing the snail gland product to ultraviolet light, the dye produced was identical in appearance to the plant dye, Indigo tinctoria. Even more impressive, molecular analysis revealed that both of these dyes had exactly the same molecular structure[30]

The Temple Institute has already made a fine supply of this requisite blue dye and has used it to properly color the beautiful newly tailored priestly robes. God's providential intervention is always at work.

Before proceeding on to the next sign of the end times, it is worth briefly discussing one of the other necessary dye colors for the priests' garments, that is, the specific dye required to stain the appropriate garment a crimson red. The Temple Institute's leader, Rabbi Chaim Richman, led a group of interested people into the village of Neve Tsuf, Samaria on July 16, 2008 to harvest the tola'at shani, also known as the crimson worm. The purpose for that gathering was to harvest enough worms to produce adequate dye for the staining of the sixteen meter long belts of the priestly garments that were being readied for use in the future Third Temple. Like the Murex trunculus snail, this worm has also been recently rediscovered in the land of Israel. The required crimson dye is easily obtained from that worm – and only that worm. However, it requires a significant number of worms to make the needed quantity of dye for all of the priests' garments. Therefore, additional trips to harvest more worms will be conducted at regular intervals until all necessary garments have been made and colored properly.

There is an intriguing story behind the life cycle of these little creatures. As death approaches for the female worm, she climbs a tree and firmly attaches her body to it. Eventually, she will lay her eggs and deposit them underneath her body to protect them from predators. After the larvae hatch, they will be fed via the ultimate sacrifice of their mother. As she dies, this mother worm secretes a crimson fluid from within her body. This red fluid stains her body and those of her infants. Because of her sacrifice, her offspring gain life. It is a wonderful reminder of how the shedding of the blood of our Savior while He was up on that cross at Calvary was able to give life to all those who desire to be a member of His family.[31]

King David put it this way when he described the agony of the cross that His Savior would one day endure ... "But I am a worm and not a man, scorned by men and despised by the people. [7] All who see me mock me; they hurl insults, shaking their heads" (Psalms 22:6-7). It is very interesting to note that the Hebrew word that David used for "worm" in the verse above is the same word that is used for the crimson worm. He was referring to that future day when Jesus Christ would shed His blood while impaled on a tree as a sacrifice for all those who would only believe on Him.

It is quite intriguing how God has even used the dyes for the garments of the priests as signs of the soon coming of His Son. It has been almost two thousand years since these colors were available for use, but they are available today. In fact, virtually everything is set for the rebuilding, refurnishing and reuse of the Temple. Never before in history has this been the case.

24. A Red Heifer without Blemish Must Be Born and Sacrificed to Purify the Temple in Israel:

The LORD said to Moses and Aaron:[2] "**This is a requirement of the law that the Lord has commanded: Tell the Israelites to bring you a red heifer without defect or blemish and that has never been under a yoke.**[3] Give it to

Eleazar the priest; it is to be taken outside the camp and slaughtered in his presence.[4] Then Eleazar the priest is to take some of its blood on his finger and sprinkle it seven times toward the front of the Tent of Meeting.[5] While he watches, **the heifer is to be burned--its hide, flesh, blood and offal.**[6] The priest is to take some cedar wood, hyssop and scarlet wool and throw them onto the burning heifer.[7] After that, the priest must wash his clothes and bathe himself with water. He may then come into the camp, but he will be ceremonially unclean till evening.[8] The man who burns it must also wash his clothes and bathe with water, and he too will be unclean till evening.[9] **"A man who is clean shall gather up the ashes of the heifer and put them in a ceremonially clean place outside the camp. They shall be kept by the Israelite community for use in the water of cleansing; it is for purification from sin."** (Num 19:1-9)

This is a very interesting sign. Ezekiel notes that the Israelites will be gathered together from all the nations into which they have been scattered, and then brought back into their Promised Land. Prior to their resumption of proper worship, they will need proper ceremonial cleansing, as will the new Temple that they will build for worship and meeting with God. Unfortunately, ashes of a "perfect" red heifer are needed for this ceremonial cleansing, and their whereabouts are currently unknown. In fact, the Copper Scroll that was found in 1952 stated that the last offering of the sacrifice of the red heifer was in A.D. 68. Two years later, Jerusalem was attacked by the Romans. Prior to this attack, priests were able to hide the ashes along with other important items and bury them for later use. However, as already noted, no one today knows their current location. Interestingly, directions are given in the scroll concerning where to look for the buried goods. Given the changes in terrain in the past two thousand years and the somewhat nebulous instructions, the directions have so far been too difficult to follow. Of course, that may well change as the search continues.

Regardless of the current situation concerning the hidden ashes from long ago, in the Old Testament Scriptures, God states that certain rites of purification are required to dedicate the Temple of the Lord. Since a new Temple will be built prior to the midpoint of the coming Tribulation, it is obvious that whatever is needed for proper ceremonial cleansing must be available by that time. The Temple and the ancient stones on the Temple Mount (which have been defiled by blood over the centuries) both need to be cleansed via a specific ritual cleansing. An unblemished red heifer is needed. Moses Maimonides (the great Jewish rabbi and Torah scholar of the twelfth century) believed that there were only nine red (spotless) heifers ever used in the making of the ashes. He said that *the tenth one would come on the scene only when the Messiah was ready to appear.*

Therefore, if we are living in times that are close to the second coming of Christ, it would make good sense if the ashes of a spotless red heifer would soon come onto the scene. The people in the Jewish Temple Institute clearly understand the need for this special animal. In fact, since the 1990s, several red cattle have been bred in hopes that one will be born without a blemish of any kind. There have been a couple of occasions where it looked like a perfect red heifer had been born, only to have a slight defect appear after the animal had aged for two to three years. In fact, in the early years of the twenty-first century, Rabbi Chaim Reichman, director of the Temple Institute even certified one of these animals just a short time before it showed its color defect. Unfortunately, in an area that had been bruised, a few white hairs began to grow. As the years passed, at a ranch in Mt. Carmel, cattle continued to be bred, waiting for the necessary red heifer – the one born a pure red color and without one blemish. Other breeding sites also continued the watch for this much anticipated birth.

Amazingly, on March 2, 2010, Rabbi Chaim began his weekly radio show by telling his audience that he had a "bombshell" announcement. He then reported the following, "The bombshell that I wanted to mention is the fact that because everyone is very interested in the status of the red heifer... and there is a tradition that the tenth red heifer is the one that is associated with the rebuilding of the Third Temple... I wanted to share with our listeners far and wide the fact that there is definitely a kosher red heifer here in Israel." When his co-host, Yitzchak Reuven suggested that this should be major news on CNN, Reichman responded, "It should be. We're not making a lot of noise about it. We're not taking out a lot of ads and we're certainly not disclosing the location. That's definitely not prudent and I'm not going to be sharing this information with the United States Embassy. But, you should know that there is definitely at least one... in fact, I think there is more than one... kosher red heifer here in Israel right now. That is not what is impeding the process now."[32] That last comment meant that there were other political reasons why the Temple was not yet being built. The red heifer was now ready to play its very important role. Purification of the Temple mount and the Temple will now be possible.

Figure 5: Jewish Priest in his Beautiful Robe and Various Temple Utensils

Figure 6: The Ark of the Covenant

Figure 7: The Menorah

Chapter 5

ISRAEL WILL BE INVOLVED IN MANY WARS IN THE END TIMES

ANYONE WHO follows current events knows that Israel has many bellicose enemies. This fact is particularly unfortunate as this little nation has gone out of their way to avoid war. Unfortunately, there have already been several occasions since 1948 where war has been forced upon them. Not only did they have to fight to keep their newfound independence in 1948, but they also were involved in costly wars in 1956, 1967, 1973, 1982, 1991, and 2006. G o d prophesied that in the latter days, Israel would be surrounded by enemy nations and involved in numerous battles. These wars would involve a great many Middle Eastern nations as well as several nations in Africa, the Far East, Russia, Iran, and others. Mention is made by several Old Testament prophets about these wars. Isaiah, Asaph, Ezekiel, Zephaniah, Zechariah, Daniel, Obadiah, and others were given dreams and visions by God detailing the combatants and the outcome of these wars. The Apostle John was also given a detailed vision about the wars that will take place during the Tribulation. The Revelation of Jesus Christ is a detailed prophecy about this seven year period of judgment.

Although no one should be dogmatic when writing about when and exactly which countries will do battle with Israel, there is a general consensus among prophecy scholars concerning some of the basics. For example, many believe that the war between the nations listed as coming against Israel in Psalm 83 will take place just before, or immediately after, the Rapture of the church. Israel will win that war. Then, the infamous Ezekiel 38/39 war likely will follow soon after this Israeli victory and prior to the halfway mark of the Tribulation. Once again, Israel will be victorious. Late in the Tribulation, the economic center of the Antichrist, Babylon, will be crushed. The one war that Israel will be in marked danger of losing, the Battle of Armageddon, will come at the conclusion of the Great Tribulation. Armies from all corners of the earth, including a 200 million man army from China and the Far East will invade that little nation. Just before Israel is crushed by the Antichrist and His armies, Jesus will return to earth with His saints to quickly and easily claim victory. Satan and His minions will be defeated. The glorious Millennial Kingdom will begin very soon thereafter.

One very amazing fact concerning all of these wars is that Israel will be victorious in every one of them. God said that He will protect Israel during these end-time wars and not allow any foreign nation to defeat His chosen people. It is possible that they may lose a small skirmish or two, but no enemy will ever defeat them in a significant war. Israel will remain in possession of their nation until the Second Coming… and beyond, into the Millennium. Now, let us take a look at some of the nations that will come against Israel in the years not very far in the future.

25. In the Last Days, Israel Will Be Surrounded by Arab Enemy Nations:

Israel is surrounded today by many nations that have as their goal the complete annihilation of the Jewish people. It is strange that such a tiny nation can illicit such antipathy from so many people. However, that is exactly the situation that was prophesied to exist in the latter days. This very unfortunate antagonistic situation began over four thousand years ago. It was the result of Abraham and his wife, Sarah, not having the patience to wait on a very important promise from God.

Abraham was the man that God chose to father the nation of Israel. The people making up this nation were to be known as the chosen people of God. Abraham and Sarah waited for the birth of a son. They waited for what they thought was a very long time. Sarah was in her mid-seventies. She became convinced that God was not going to honor His promise, at least in granting her a child through Abraham. She went to her husband and suggested that he "sleep" with her handmaiden, Hagar. In that way, Abraham would have his heir. Arrangements of that type were not that unusual in those days and in that culture. Hagar soon gave birth to Abraham's first son. Abraham was eighty-six years old. The infant was given the name Ishmael. However, he was not to be the son of promise.

Thirteen years later, when Abraham was ninety-nine years old, God told him that Sarah would now conceive and give birth to the child promised so long ago. Both Abraham and Sarah laughed at the idea. One year later, their first son was born. They named him Isaac, which means "laughter" in Hebrew. Isaac later fathered Jacob and Esau. Jacob, the grandson of Abraham, fathered twelve sons, giving rise to the twelve tribes of Israel.

Ishmael was in his teens when Isaac was born to Abraham and Sarah. Tensions arose between Sarah, Hagar, and Ishmael. Because of that uncomfortable situation, Sarah asked Abraham to tell Hagar to leave and to take Ishmael along. Abraham was distressed as he did not want to lose his oldest son. However, he did honor his wife's request, but not before being given the promise that God would make a great nation from the descendants of Ishmael. Even before Hagar had given birth, God had promised her the same thing. The result is that many of the modern day Arabs are descendants of Ishmael.

One other very important result of this whole unusual situation is that the Lord God prophesied that the heirs of Ishmael would always be at odds with the heirs of Isaac. Both would be the father of many people, but there would be enmity between the Arabs and the Israelites (Jews). During Old Testament times, the nations that were made up of the progeny of Ishmael were often at odds with Israel, just as prophesied below…

> The angel added, "**I will so increase your descendants [Hagar's descendents] that they will be too numerous to count.**"[11] The angel of the LORD also said to her: "You are now with child and you will have a son. You shall name him Ishmael, for the LORD has heard of your misery. [12] **He will be a wild donkey of a man; his hand will be against everyone and everyone's hand against him, and he will live in hostility toward all his brothers.**" (Gen 16:10-12)

During the time of King David, the prophet Asaph wrote the Psalm that appears below. He told of the coming day when Israel would be surrounded by many enemy nations that would come against them from all sides. The prophet called on God to help His "people" in the ensuing conflict. He asked God to pursue the enemy, frighten them, and shame them, so that these enemy forces might know without any question that the God of Israel was the Lord, Most High, over all of the earth.

Israel was surrounded by enemies as described by Asaph during the times that he wrote. There are Bible commentators who view Psalm 83 as referencing only the times back in the Kingdom Age of Israel. Lately however, there are many prophecy scholars who see an eerie similarity between the nations that are mentioned in this Psalm and the nations that currently threaten Israel. Very possibly, as is true with so many of Old Testament prophecies, God planned a true and proper fulfillment for this prophecy for the time not long after Asaph lived as well as a future fulfillment in the latter days.

Certainly it is true, that a straight forward study of current events shows that the nations that Asaph alluded to will very likely be involved in a future conflict with Israel. The prophecy follows:

> O God, do not keep silent; be not quiet, O God, be not still.² **See how your enemies are astir, how your foes rear their heads.**³ With cunning they conspire against your people; they plot against those you cherish.⁴ **"Come," they say, "let us destroy them as a nation, that the name of Israel be remembered no more."** ⁵ With one mind they plot together; **they form an alliance against you--** ⁶ **the tents of Edom and the Ishmaelites, of Moab and the Hagrites,**⁷ **Gebal, Ammon and Amalek, Philistia, with the people of Tyre.** ⁸ **Even Assyria** has joined them to lend strength to the descendants of Lot. (Psalms 83:1-8)

> **So pursue them with your tempest and terrify them with your storm.** ¹⁶ **Cover their faces with shame so that men will seek your name, O Lord.** ¹⁷ May they ever be ashamed and dismayed; may they perish in disgrace.¹⁸ Let them know that you, whose name is the LORD-- that you alone are the Most High over all the earth. (Psalms 83:15-18)

Here are the locations for each of the nations mentioned above:

- Edom and the Ishmaelites – located south and southeast of the Dead Sea
- Moab – located east of the Dead Sea, north of Edom
- Hagrites – located east of the Dead Sea
- Gebal – current day Lebanon
- Ammon – located east of the Dead Sea, just north of Moab
- Amalek – located southeast of Israel

- Philistia – located on the coast of the Mediterranean Sea – south-central modern day Israel
- Tyre – located on the coast of the Mediterranean Sea just north of Galilee (may include Lebanon)
- Assyria – north of Israel, includes modern day Syria and portions of Iran and Iraq

There are several other places in the Old Testament that also state that Israel will be surrounded by Arabic enemy nations in the end times. Two of the more intriguing are found in the book of Isaiah. The first of these relates to coming events in Syria, the second involves Egypt.

- Syria: An oracle concerning Damascus: "See, **Damascus will no longer be a city but will become a heap of ruins… In the evening, sudden terror! Before the morning, they are gone!**" (Isaiah 17:1&14)

Damascus, Syria has never before in its history been destroyed. Certainly, it never has become "a heap of ruins." Therefore, this prophecy must be meant for some time in the future. Imagine just how quickly a nuclear attack could destroy a city. The verse above may very well be a description of this kind of attack.

There has been mounting evidence over the past few years that Syria has accumulated a significant arsenal of weapons of mass destruction (WMD). There is little doubt that they possess biological and chemical weapons ready for use. They were so close to having nuclear weapons that Israel had to make a preemptive first strike on a nuclear reactor site in northeast Syria on September 6, 2007. However, there has been good evidence gained since that time, that Syria has up to four nuclear facilities besides the one hit by Israel five years ago. The Institute for Science and International Security (ISIS) has stated recently that they believe Syria is far more advanced in nuclear capabilities than previously thought. ISIS chief, David Albright, said that there is significant evidence that truck convoys took WMDs into Syria from Iraq in the weeks just before the war with Iraq began. "The man who served as the no. 2 official in Saddam Hussein's air force says Iraq moved weapons of mass destruction into Syria before the war by loading the weapons into civilian aircraft in which the passenger seats were removed."[33] The report went on to say that there were fifty-six total flights in all. Ali Hussein was in charge of this operation. He was known as "Chemical Ali." Many in the Israeli and United States intelligence community are very concerned about these reports of Syria possessing nuclear, chemical, and biological weapons. Of course, Israel is keeping a wary eye on that nation.

A civil war erupted in Syria in early 2011 as part of the wider Arab Spring. Just as was the case in many other Middle Eastern and African nations, the people in Syria have grown tired of their oppressive dictatorial government under Bashar al-Assad. This conflict continued to escalate during the summer of 2012. Russia and China are standing behind the current regime while the United States and the European Union have condemned the violence against the civilian protesters. This situation is a powder-keg ready to explode.

Hal Lindsey suggests that the biblical prophecy noted in Isaiah 17 implies an exchange between Israel and Damascus (or possibly a preemptive first strike by Israel on Damascus) that will result in the destruction of Damascus and the beginning of the Psalm 83 war. This is a reasonable scenario considering the current geopolitical situation in the Middle East and the prophecy of Isaiah and Asaph in Psalm 83.

- Egypt: In a television show prior to 2011, prophecy teacher Perry Stone spoke of a likely civil war within the nation of Egypt. He got this idea from reading the prophecies in Isaiah

19. It is interesting that Egypt did engage in a civil war soon after Perry's prediction. Note Isaiah's prophecy...

"I will stir up Egyptian against Egyptian-- brother will fight against brother, neighbor against neighbor, city against city" (Isaiah 19:2).

The prophecy continues with, "I will hand the Egyptians over to the power of a cruel master, and a fierce king will rule over them," declares the Lord, the LORD Almighty (Isaiah 19:4).

On December 18, 2010, a revolution began in the North African nation of Tunisia. Within four weeks, their president, Zine El Abidine Ben Ali, fled to Saudi Arabia in defeat. In late January 25, 2011, a civil war in Egypt erupted. Their President, Hosni Mubarak, was forced to resign from office on February 11, 2011. This civil war was followed by the overthrow of the Libyan leader, the infamous Muammar Gaddafi in August. These and several additional uprisings in Arab nations in 2011 became known as the Arab Spring. The hope of the free world was that peaceful and democratic governments would arise out of this popular unrest and strife.

However, many are very concerned that the Muslim Brotherhood may take over in many of these countries. The Obama administration remains optimistic as evidenced by the report given by James Clapper, director of National Intelligence, in February of 2011 while testifying in front of a congressional committee on just this topic. He said, "The term 'Muslim Brotherhood' is an umbrella term for a variety of movements, in the case of Egypt, a very heterogeneous group, largely secular, which has eschewed violence and has decried Al Qaeda as a perversion of Islam... They have pursued social ends, a betterment of the political order in Egypt, et cetera... In other countries, there is no overarching agenda, particularly in pursuit of violence, at least internationally." Unfortunately, there are many who would disagree with his assessment, including the leaders of that very organization. Please consider the following:

- Hamas is the Palestinian branch of the Brotherhood. Hamas is a known terrorist group that launches bombs into Israel from Gaza practically every day.
- Several infamous terrorists, including Osama Bin Laden, are or were members of this brotherhood.
- Representative Sue Myrick said in response to the comments of James Clapper, "The danger of the Muslim Brotherhood is not just encouraging terrorism through their ideology, but also to take over governments so everyone has to succumb and live under their ideology."[34]
- "The Brotherhood is close to achieving the 'ultimate goal' set by the group's founder Hasan al Banna in 1928, which is the establishment of a 'just and reasonable regime.'"[35] The regime of which he speaks is a caliphate wherein Islam rules the entire world.
- The Muslim Brotherhood Supreme Guide, Muhammad Badi, declared jihad against "the Muslim's real enemies, not only Israel but also the United States. Waging jihad against both of these infidels is a commandment of Allah that cannot be disregarded."[36]
- In January 2012 the deputy leader of the Muslim Brotherhood, Rashad al-Bayoumi, said that the Muslim Brotherhood "did not sign the peace accords [with Israel] . . . . To me, it isn't binding at all . . . . On no condition will we recognize Israel. It is an enemy entity . . . . We won't cooperate with Israel in any situation."[37]
- Muslim Brotherhood spiritual leader Yusuf al-Qaradawi said, "Today the Jews are not the Israelites praised by Allah, but the descendants of the Israelites who defied His word. Allah was angry with them and turned them into monkeys

and pigs... There is no doubt that the battle in which the Muslims overcome the Jews [will come] . . . . In that battle the Muslims will fight the Jews and kill them."[38]

- On a television speech on January 30, 2009, Sheikh Yusuf Qaradawi also said, "Throughout history, Allah has imposed upon the [Jews] people who would punish them for their corruption. The last punishment was carried out by Hitler. By means of all the things he did to them – even though they exaggerated this issue – he managed to put them in their place. This was divine punishment for them. Allah willing, the next time will be at the hand of the believers."[39]

The question still remains, however, whether the Muslim Brotherhood will gain a foothold in these nations that have just undergone revolution. For instance, will Egypt be eventually taken over by the caliphate and ruled by Islamic Law? Unfortunately, events are certainly going in that direction. The Muslim Brotherhood won the January 2012 parliamentary elections in Egypt with 47% of the vote. The hard line Islamic Salafis faction garnered 24%. Therefore, the combined vote for Islamic rule was 71% of the total. In June Mohamed Morsi was elected president of Egypt after receiving 52% of the vote. He represented Egypt's Freedom and Justice Party, the political component of the Muslim Brotherhood. "He previously told CNN he'd honor Egypt's 1979 accord with Israel, but in the past, the Islamist figure has referred to Israeli leaders as 'vampires.'"[40] It surely looks like the Muslim Brotherhood has already taken control of that country.

Not only Egypt, but Tunisia, Libya, Morocco, and Yemen have also had their elections dominated by the Muslim brotherhood. All of these countries now will be influenced by this Islamic jihad group. Syria, Jordan, Algeria, Saudi Arabia and several other nations are at serious risk in the region. There is no doubt that the nation of Israel is very concerned about the recent turn of events in Egypt along with all of the other nations now being influenced by the Muslim Brotherhood.

Jordan occupies a portion of the land area that is mentioned as being an enemy of Israel in the latter days. Obed Eran of the Institute for National Securities Studies is greatly concerned that the so-called Arab Spring may bring the Muslim Brotherhood to leadership in that nation as well, "Within the Kingdom and across three of its borders, unfolding developments carry far reaching implications for the region in general and Jordan's stability in particular."[41] Refugees from Iraq, Syria and the Palestinian Authority in the Muslim Brotherhood hope that they may one day soon rise to power in Jordan as they did in so many other nations in 2011.

In summary, the nations that today represent the ancient countries prophesied to surround Israel in the end times include: Lebanon, Egypt, Syria, Jordan, and the Palestinian territories within Israel. Each of these modern day nations have reason to want Israel defeated. Frankly, most have a long standing animus toward the Jews and their nation just as Asaph noted so very long ago. They believe that the nation of Israel should not exist. One way or another, the followers of Allah want to eliminate Israel. Even if this were not prophesied to happen in the Bible, common sense would lead most reasonably intelligent people to this conclusion. Given the enemy, nuclear war is a very likely possibility. If this Psalm does have prophetic significance, and this is considered likely by many, it will be interesting to see the future interactions between all of the nations mentioned above. For example, will Jordan soon fall victim to the Muslim Brotherhood? What is going to happen in Syria? God told His people and the world through His Holy Word that Israel would be hated through the ages by other nations… and they certainly have been. He also said that in the end times they would be surrounded by enemy Arab nations, and they are.

In the next sign, another group of nations that will one day come against Israel near the onset of the Tribulation will be reviewed.

This is often referred to as the Ezekiel 38/39 War. Many believe that the war described by the prophet Ezekiel will come soon *after* the war suggested by Psalm 83. As far as the timing is concerned, only God knows for sure. However, God did tell us that the war itself was a future certainty.

26. There will be a Major Conflict Between Russia, Iran and Several of the Nations Surrounding Israel:

The most devastating war in history will be waged as the seven year Tribulation draws to a close. Nations from all over the world will come against Israel at this time. The war will take place in the valley of Megiddo, which is located in Israel; this war is commonly referred to as the Battle of Armageddon. Just before the world is destroyed, the Lord Jesus will return with His saints to defeat the Antichrist and the forces of evil. This Second Coming will usher in the Millennial Kingdom, a beautiful thousand year period on earth where Jesus will reign supreme. The Apostle John was given a vision of this future period on earth while he was banished on the Isle of Patmos as the first century drew to a close. This he wrote about in the book, The Revelation of Jesus Christ...

> I saw heaven standing open and there before me was a white horse, whose rider is called Faithful and True. With justice He judges and makes war.[12] His eyes are like blazing fire, and on His head are many crowns. He has a name written on him that no one knows but He himself.[13] He is dressed in a robe dipped in blood, and His name is the Word of God.[14] The armies of heaven were following Him, riding on white horses and dressed in fine linen, white and clean.[15] Out of His mouth comes a sharp sword with which to strike down the nations. "He will rule them with an iron scepter." (Rev 19:11-15)

Prior to this "war of wars," there will be at least two or three other wars during the Tribulation. Psalm 83 and Isaiah 17 and 19, previously discussed, list the enemy nations that will attack Israel near the onset of this seven year period. At least this timing is what most prophecy scholars suggest. Another war, often referred to as the Ezekiel 38/39 war, will also likely take place in the early years of the Tribulation. As will soon be seen, many of the nations that attack Israel in the Psalm 83 war will not apparently be involved in the Ezekiel war. It may well be that since these Arab nations will be soundly defeated by Israel in that earlier war, they will be in no position to join with Russia and Iran in the next war. This war is described by the prophet Ezekiel as follows:

> The word of the LORD came to me: ² "Son of man, set your face against Gog, of the **land of Magog,** the chief prince of **Meshech** and **Tubal**; prophesy against him ³ and say: 'This is what the Sovereign LORD says: I am against you, O Gog, chief prince of Meshech and Tubal. ⁴ **I will turn you around, put hooks in your jaws and bring you out** with your whole army--your horses, your horsemen fully armed, and a great horde with large and small shields, all of them brandishing their swords. ⁵ **Persia, Cush** and **Put** will be with them, all with shields and helmets, ⁶ also **Gomer** with all its troops, and **Beth Togarmah** from the far north with all its troops--the **many nations with you.** ⁷ Get ready; be prepared, you and all the hordes gathered about you, and take command of them. 8 After many days you will be called to arms. **In future years you will invade a land that has recovered from war, whose people were gathered from many nations to the mountains of Israel, which had long been desolate.** They had been brought out from the nations, and now all of them live in safety.⁹ **You and all your troops and the many nations with you will go up, advancing like a storm; you will be like a cloud covering the land.**¹⁰ 'This is what the

Sovereign LORD says: On that day thoughts will come into your mind and you will devise an evil scheme.[11] You will say, "**I will invade a land of unwalled villages**; I will attack a peaceful and unsuspecting people--all of them living without walls and without gates and bars.[12] **I will plunder and loot and turn my hand against the resettled ruins and the people gathered from the nations, rich in livestock and goods, living at the center of the land.**'" (Ezek 38:1-12)

You will advance against my people Israel like a cloud that covers the land. **In days to come, O Gog, I will bring you against my land, so that the nations may know me when I show myself holy through you before their eyes.** [17] "This is what the Sovereign LORD says: Are you not the one I spoke of in former days by my servants the prophets of Israel? At that time they prophesied for years that I would bring you against them. [18] This is what will happen in that day: **When Gog attacks the land of Israel, my hot anger will be aroused, declares the Sovereign Lord.**" (Ezek 38:16-18)

The verses above were written down by the prophet Ezekiel almost 2,600 years ago. He wrote concerning the end times on this earth just before the Tribulation would begin. In the previous chapter (Ezekiel 37), the prophet wrote about the return of the Jewish people to Israel using the "word picture" of bones and sinews coming together to depict the nation of Israel's rebirth in the latter days. In this next chapter, he warned of the gathering of a coalition of many nations that would come against Israel in war. Interestingly, God pointed out that He would ultimately be behind this war ("**I will turn you around, put hooks into your jaws, and bring you out**") as He was going to use this war for His glory and to bring Israel back to where they belonged... trusting in God and knowing that Jesus was their true Messiah.

There has been much written by prophecy teachers in the past several decades about this future war and the alignment of nations that will make up the coalition against Israel. Today, the evaluation of that topic proves very interesting indeed. Joel Rosenberg has recently written a best-seller titled, *The Ezekiel Option* in which he took the prophecy of Ezekiel 38 and turned it into an exciting novel. His non-fiction book, *Epicenter*, may even be more interesting as it goes into factual details showing how much of the Middle East political situation is shaping up to suggest that the war predicted in this thirty-eighth chapter of Ezekiel may not be very far off in the future. It is interesting to read about the thought processes behind the writing of Rosenberg's book. For example, when he first began to write a book on the end times, he wondered about the fact that Iraq was not mentioned in these verses in Ezekiel. At the time, Saddam Hussein was still in his ignominious glory, a powerful figure in the region, with a marked hatred of Israel. It was very difficult to imagine a war involving many of the Arab nations, Russia, and Iran, but excluding Iraq. It was going to be difficult, he thought, to write a believable book without involving Iraq in this future Russia/Iran/Arab war. Then came September 11, 2001. Now, several years have gone by, and Iraq is a fledgling democracy and ally of the United States. Today, the setting described in Ezekiel 38 has just about all come together.

Now, let us take a look at the nations that will come against Israel… and lose:

- Magog – Russia (Gog is the ruler of Magog and leader of the invasion)
- Rosh – modern day Russian people and some of the former Soviet republics
- Meshech, Tubal, Beth-Togarmah, and Gomer – all are parts of modern day Turkey
- Persia – Iran

- Cush – Northern Sudan, Ethiopia
- Put – Northern Libya, Algeria, Tunisia
- Many peoples with you – most likely, nearby Islamic allies

Ed Hindson and Tim LaHaye say that this prophecy is "most likely a prophecy of a 'Russian'- led invasion of Israel....Which parts of 'Russia' may be a matter of debate, but Russia's involvement in this invasion is clearly indicated."[42] The reason quote marks are placed around Russia is that these men are not sure which parts of the former Soviet Union and current day Russia correspond to the Rosh and Magog of 2,500 years ago. In any case, the modern nation known as Russia will be a major player in this invasion force.

Given all of the other nations noted, Israel will be attacked by a massive enemy contingent. All of these nations are currently either very anti-Israel or moving in that direction quickly. For example, in November 2002, Turkey elected a pro-Islamic party to govern the country. Unfortunately for Israel, this nation has continued to move toward an anti-Israel stance since that time. For example, just recently, "Turkish sources reported that Turkish Prime Minister, Receb Tayyip Erdogan, sent a confidential letter to Ismail Haniyya, Prime Minister of the Hamas-led government in the Gaza Strip, inviting him to visit Turkey, and informing him that he decided to grant the government $300 million."[43]

Now Turkey is even involved with treaty conversations with Iran. Since the so-called Arab Spring discussed earlier, Libya and the Sudan are now being dominated by the Muslim Brotherhood, an avowed enemy of Israel. Russia signed a multi-billion dollar arms deal with Libya in 2008. They are also strengthening ties with Turkey. All of the other nations listed above have been anti-Semitic for a long time.

In order to better understand the background that will lead up to Russia joining forces with Iran in an invasion of Israel, it is important to recognize what has happened between these two nations in the last couple of decades. Prior to the collapse of communism, the relationship between Iran and Russia had been strained at best for centuries. However, with the breakup of the Soviet Union, Russia's needs and interests have changed. Especially since Putin came into power, Russia and Iran have found that they have much to offer each other.

After many of the countries that formerly made up the Soviet Union broke away, Russia found itself in significant economic distress. No longer considered a super power, they still wanted to remain an important nation on the world scene. They needed to build up their economy, and they wanted to regain some of their lost influence in foreign policy matters. Iran was the perfect fit. Each of these nations needed each other. Russia sold Iran a great deal of their aircraft and military inventory. They also have provided them with much sought after military, energy, and nuclear technology. Russia is also an important ally in their quest for a nuclear weapon as they try to fend off the United States and their allies. For example, in early 2012, "Russia's Foreign Minister, Sergei Lavrov, vowed to veto any United Nations proposal for military intervention in Syria and promised especially to do all they could to prevent a military strike on Iran. 'The consequences [of attacking Iran] will be extremely grave,' he said. 'It's not going to be an easy walk. It will trigger a chain reaction and I don't know where it will stop.' Russia has even been training its military on scenarios related to the crisis of a possible military conflict in Iran."[44] In January, 2012, the outgoing Russian ambassador to NATO, Dmitry Rogozin, said, "Iran is our neighbor, and if Iran is involved in any military action, it is a direct threat to our security."[45]

Russia gets much from its new relationship with Iran as well. Iran has provided Russia with a significant economic boost including jobs for their scientists, a significant market for their products, access to oil, influence over competing Muslim nations, and respect from other nations of the world. Russia is once again a very important player in international politics.

Some may wonder why Russia would attack Israel. For one thing, as shown in an earlier discussion, Israel has more national treasure to offer each year. For another, as just noted, Russia is now an important ally of Iran. Iran, with their current leadership, is very much looking forward to attacking their arch-enemy, Israel.

President Mahmoud Ahmadinejad and the current Iranian Ayatollah, Ali Khamenei, have a very interesting reason for wanting to start a war with Israel... and the sooner the better. To understand the reason for the hawkish attitude of these two leaders of Iran, one must understand their religious beliefs. Both of these leaders belong to a small sect of Shia Islam. They are Shiite Islamic Fanatics. They are called Twelvers. A Twelver believes that it is their duty to create the conditions which will bring back the 12th Imam. He is their Messiah. These conditions require a mass carnage of Jews and Christians through war against Islamic nations. Of course, they are convinced that this would be exactly the situation that would occur when they acquire a nuclear weapon and launch it against Israel. Since the coming of this Twelfth Imam (also known as the Mahdi) will result in a glorious Islamic victory... they are not worried about any other outcome.

There are varying stories of the Mahdi. He supposedly was born in A.D. 868 (some propose a different date for his birth). His father, the eleventh Imam, died on 1 January A.D. 874. Soon after the death of his father, the young child, the Twelfth Imam, disappeared from the earth. There are different opinions as to exactly when and how this happened. Many say he disappeared into a well in Jamkaran, Iran. He did this through what Muslims refer to as going into occultation, some form of suspended state. Allah was behind this disappearance. That is what Ahmadinejad believes. The Iranian president has poured millions of dollars into building the beautiful Jamkaran Mosque to house this well. He has been building a connecting road to allow for easy access from the Mosque to Tehran when the Mahdi reappears out of the well upon his return to earth. Very soon after the Mahdi returns to earth, so will his "right hand man," Jesus Christ. At that time, Jesus will reveal to all Jews and Christians their massive error in rejecting Islam. They will have the opportunity to repent. However, if they do not, they will suffer the fate of all those who reject Allah. Soon after his return, the Mahdi will usher in a perfect world of peace and harmony for all good Muslims.

Ahmadinejad has repeatedly said that Allah directed him to prepare the way for the coming of the Mahdi. Khamenei said that he met with the Twelfth Imam (he did not speak of the nature of this visit). Mesbah Yazdi, one of Iran's leading advocates of Islamic end-times ideology, recently spoke on that topic. CBN News recently reported "the Mahdi will return to slaughter all non-Muslims and establish a global Islamic empire. Yazdi, who is a mentor to Ahmadinejad, has gave Khamenei his apocalyptic stamp of approval. Yazdi also stated that Khamenei ascends to the sky every year for five hours, meeting with Imam Mahdi … They are defending the Supreme Leader's position as a saint, as a prophet, as the one who is going to pass the flag of Islam to Imam Mahdi. Judging by its recent statements and actions, the Iranian government believes that day is coming very soon."[46]

Therefore, both of these leaders are working to prepare the way for this false messiah. To do so, the world must be in a state of chaos. Hence, they have this ambitious plan to attack Israel and the West with all of the force they can muster. This attack, apparently, must include nuclear weapons. Iran will one day soon join forces with their allies, Russia, and several like-minded Arab nations and attack Israel. Most experts believe that Iran will successfully develop their own nuclear weapons sometime between 2013 and 2015. With the technology that they receive from nations such as North Korea, Russia, and China, they likely will be able to launch an attack on mainland United States within five years. This could be done by using an offshore freighter, scuttling the ship after the missile launch.

It is interesting to note a couple of the nations that are not mentioned in Ezekiel's prophecy - Iraq and Afghanistan. As we know, Iraq is now a fledgling democracy, and the fundamentalist Islamic malcontents in Afghanistan are being kept at bay by the United States. Thus, all of the nations prophesied to come against Israel have aligned against them at this time. The nations that are located nearby Israel that are not mentioned in Ezekiel's prophecy (for example, Iraq) also make sense. All is ready, all is in place, awaiting God's unknowable, perfect timing.

Without God's support, victory in this war would be impossible. However, God will ensure that Israel will win this war. It is likely that this war will follow a short time after the Psalm 83 war. The Bible does not make the timing of these two wars clear. However, both are very likely to come prior to the midpoint of the Tribulation. Suffice it to say, most scholars believe this battle will come at least a few years before the Battle of Armageddon.

27. A 200,000,000 Man Army Will March Against Israel at Some Point During the Tribulation:

> The sixth angel sounded his trumpet, and I heard a voice coming from the horns of the golden altar that is before God.[14] It said to the sixth angel who had the trumpet, "**Release the four angels who are bound at the great river Euphrates.**"[15] And the four angels who had been kept ready for this very hour and day and month and year were released to kill a third of mankind.[16] **The number of the mounted troops was two hundred million.** I heard their number. (Rev 9:13-16)

Here we see that during the Great Tribulation a vast army of 200 million will march against Israel. This was not going to happen during the time of Christ as there were no armies even approaching that size. Historians say that there were less than 450 million people in the entire world at that time. In days gone by, people often would interpret this verse (and many others as we have noted before) figuratively. For example, some suggested that this was simply alluding to a very large fighting force.

Today, however, it looks far more likely that God actually did mean that 200 million men would come against Israel from the East in the last days. China and North Korea can easily amass an army composed of that many men.

It is also very interesting that the government of Red China has spent enormous sums of money to build a highway across Asia that heads directly toward Israel. Grant Jeffrey wrote that no foreigners are allowed near this road. "This highway has been completed, at a staggering cost of money and lives, through the rugged terrain across the south of China and through Tibet, Afghanistan, and Pakistan.[47] The question remains as to what use will it be put. The book of The Revelation has the answer. This 200,000,000 man army will one day march on this highway against Israel as the Tribulation reaches its climax. This very large army will join with other anti-Israeli and Antichrist forces in the infamous battle of Armageddon.

28. Euphrates Dries Up:

> The sixth angel poured out his bowl on the great river **Euphrates, and its water was dried up to prepare the way for the kings from the East**. (Rev 16:12)

The Euphrates River has always been a very important river, especially in biblical times. The Apostle John saw, in his vision from God in The Revelation, that this great river would be dried up in the end times in order to allow for the massive army of the kings of the east to travel into the Middle East for their war against Israel. This river has always been a virtual impassable barrier in the past. Of course, God could accomplish this task instantly should He desire. However, as noted earlier, He typically seems to act in a more providential way through seemingly "natural" means. That brings us to a recent development related to the building of dams by Turkey. A massive dam, called the Ataturk Dam, was completed in 1990. It is the fifth largest dam on earth and can hold back the great Euphrates River, allowing for the passage of an army of men from the "east." It is one mile long and 600 feet high.

A recent article in the New York Times is also of interest. The front page of the July 13, 2009 edition had the following headline, "Iraq Suffers as the Euphrates River Dwindles." It is interesting to note that even this newspaper mentioned the prophetical significance in the article. "The shrinking of the Euphrates, a river so crucial to the birth of civilization that the Book of Revelation prophesied its drying up as a sign of the end times, has decimated farms along its banks, has left fishermen impoverished and has depleted riverside towns as farmers flee to the cities looking for work."[48]

Whether the course of nature itself causes the drying up or whether the Ataturk Dam accomplishes the ultimate "drying up," for the first time in history, the Euphrates now can be crossed by a large army. Of course, these types of events are just what one would expect to happen just prior to the coming of the Messiah.

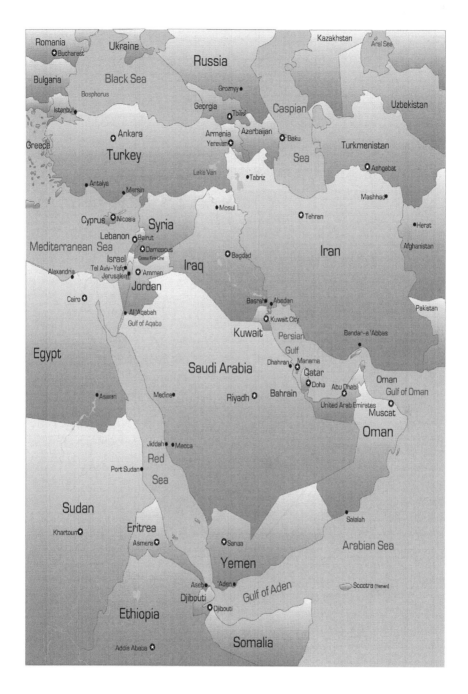

Figure 8: Map of the Middle East

Chapter 6

GOD WILL PROTECT ISRAEL IN THE LATTER DAYS

IT IS DEFINITELY true that Israel and the Jews have faced very difficult times in the years since they regained nationhood in 1948. They have fought through many wars. It is true that Israel has come out of each of these wars victorious, but they did lose many lives.

In the coming years, as was carefully noted in the previous chapter, Israel will be involved in additional wars. Some of these wars will be even more difficult, be against seemingly overwhelming odds, and will yield greater loss of life than some of these previous wars. However, one extremely important promise from God is that He will protect their nation in these end times. God will not allow Israel to lose any of these wars. Although some lives will be lost, relative to the size and strength of the opposing forces that come against them, Israel will do miraculously well.

God has already honored that promise in the many previous wars Israel has been involved in over this past sixty-five years. Many miraculous and wonderful examples are given in the first sign discussed below. This protection will be ongoing and include the final Battle of Armageddon. After Christ Jesus brings victory to

Israel during that battle, the followers of Jesus, Jews and Gentiles alike, will enter into the Millennial Kingdom.

In addition to His protection during the battles of war, God will also provide a place of refuge in Petra. The Bible mentions in more than one place that the Jews will face overwhelming odds during last half of the Tribulation. In fact, they will face death at the hands of the Antichrist unless they are able to escape from cities such as Jerusalem. Jesus tells them that they should be ready to flee into the mountains. Somehow they will need to survive with their friends and family until He comes to rescue them a few years later. One would expect that similar experiences will take place all over the globe as all those who turn to Christ during this time will face the wrath of Antichrist. In essence, it will be escape into the countryside or die.

Since there will be such a mass of dead bodies in Israel, especially after the Battle of Armageddon, God will provide help in cleaning up after the war. The help, interestingly, will be seen in the massive numbers of birds of prey that even now reside in the area where the battles will take place. More on this topic will be noted later as it is the last sign presented in this section.

29. Israel Will Remain Invincible Once It Becomes a Nation Again:

Since 1948, Israel has been attacked in three major wars and six lesser wars, yet, despite being vastly outnumbered, they have destroyed all attacking foes. Some of the stories concerning those wars have shown to almost any open-minded thinker that God had a significant hand in those victories.

There is absolutely no evidence in Old or New Testament prophecies that Israel will be defeated once they have been gathered from the four corners of the earth by God. Instead, God will bring His chosen people back to Israel and provide them with all of the other blessings that are being described within these pages. At some point in the not too distant future, after the land of Israel (including Jerusalem) is in the possession of the Jews once again, the Messiah will return to earth. Until His return God will protect Israel from foreign invasion… "the Lord will defend the inhabitants of Jerusalem" (Zech. 12:8). He will "seek to destroy all the nations that come against Jerusalem" (Zech. 12:9). Finally, a war will come at the end of the Great Tribulation during which Jesus will return to earth and provide the victory for Israel over the forces of evil. Until that time, God will bring victory to Israel using amazing providential miracles. A few examples of these miracles will be given after the biblical verses that follow…

> "On that day I will make the leaders of Judah like a firepot in a woodpile, like a flaming torch among sheaves. They will consume right and left all the surrounding peoples, but **Jerusalem will remain intact in her place.**[7] The LORD will save the dwellings of Judah first, so that the honor of the house of David and of Jerusalem's inhabitants may not be greater than that of Judah.[8] **On that day the Lord will shield those who live in Jerusalem, so that the feeblest among them will be like David, and the house of David will be like God, like the Angel of the Lord going before them.**[9] **On that day I will set out to destroy all the nations that attack Jerusalem.**[10] And I will pour out on the house of David and the inhabitants of Jerusalem a spirit of grace and supplication. **They will look on me, the one they have pierced,** and they will mourn for him as one mourns for an only child, and grieve bitterly for him as one grieves for a firstborn son." (Zech 12:6-10)

> **"The days are coming," declares the Lord, "when I will bring my people Israel and Judah back from captivity and restore them to the land I gave their forefathers to possess," says the Lord.** (Jer 30:3)

"How awful that day will be! None will be like it. It will be a time of trouble for Jacob, but he will be saved out of it."[8] "In that day," declares the LORD Almighty, "I will break the yoke off their necks and will tear off their bonds; no longer will foreigners enslave them.[9] Instead, they will serve the LORD their God." (Jer 30:7-9)

A day of the Lord is coming when your plunder will be divided among you.[2] I will gather all the nations to Jerusalem to fight against it; the city will be captured, the houses ransacked, and the women raped. Half of the city will go into exile, but the rest of the people will not be taken from the city.[3] Then the Lord will go out and fight against those nations, as he fights in the day of battle [this speaks of Armageddon when Jesus will come to save Israel].[4] On that day his feet will stand on the Mount of Olives, east of Jerusalem, and the Mount of Olives will be split in two from east to west, forming a great valley, with half of the mountain moving north and half moving south. (Zech 14:1-4)

Israel has been involved in several wars since it became a nation once again in 1948. As the Bible prophesied, God has protected them from all foreign aggression ever since. A country of only seven million people as of 2009 (and, of course, markedly less people in the 1950s and 1960s), Israel has been victorious in the 1948 War of Independence, the 1956 Suez Crisis, the very amazing 1967 Six-Day War, the War of Attrition (1968-1970), the Yom Kippur War of 1973, the Lebanon War of 1982, and they were solely responsible for taking out the Iranian Nuclear program (bombed the Osirik Reactor) in June, 1981. There was a stalemate of sorts a couple of years ago, but Israel has not lost a war since their reformation… and, the likelihood of that ever happening looks very doubtful, given what Zechariah, Jeremiah, and Ezekiel said 2,500 years ago. Since 1948, Israel has won three major wars and six smaller skirmishes against vastly greater forces; although they were sometimes outnumbered by over twenty-five to one.

Although each one of the wars that Israel has fought since their independence in 1948 has had evidence of divine intervention, the Six-Day War is replete with multiple examples. However, all of the wars that Israel has been involved in over the past six decades have had their share of miraculous, godly interventions. The following are just a few of the apparent miracles that occurred during the Six-Day War and the Yom Kippur War. An interesting example is also noted from a battle in 1958.

In the well-known war of 1967, a vastly inferior number of men with vastly inferior armaments ended up bringing victory to the forces of God. Even *Life Magazine* reported that "Israel's victory on five fronts in a short sixty hours, is absolutely astonishing."[49]

Here are some extraordinary events from that war and other recent Israeli conflicts:

1. Egypt came at Israel from the southwest, Syria from the north and Jordan from the east. Estimates were that 465,000 troops, over 2,800 tanks, and approximately 800 aircraft were ready to attack on those three borders with Israel. The rabbis in Jerusalem were readying public parks to be used as cemeteries. The Soviet Union had poured $2 billion worth of arms into the Arab nations. Israel's enemies brought at least twice as many soldiers, three times as many tanks and four times as many airplanes to the battlefield. Yet, they lost.

2. Just a few days before the war began, new and inexperienced officers were placed in command of the majority of the Egyptian brigades. Israeli planes took off on the morning of June 5, 1967. Although flying very low in an attempt to avoid detection by several enemy radar sites, Jordan did note that a large number of Israeli airplanes were heading toward

Egypt. Immediately, they sent word to Cairo concerning the attack. Providentially, the coding frequencies that the Egyptians used had been changed the previous day, so that Jordan's message of the impending attack never arrived! On that morning, Israeli planes attacked the Egyptian planes while they were still on the ground and gained an incredible victory. Over two hundred planes were destroyed. Half the Egyptian Air Force was destroyed on that first morning. Although the Israeli planes were still spotted in time for many of the Egyptian planes to escape destruction, there was a "comedy of errors" in the ranks that resulted in no one giving the command for the Egyptian pilots to get their planes in the air. Not only that, but no one gave the order to use the many available anti-aircraft guns against the advancing planes. The Israeli air force accomplished their mission with virtually no resistance. As it turned out, late the previous night the commander in chief of the Egyptian forces and many of his top officers were busy watching a belly dancer perform. This led to their not being available the next morning for the onset of some very important duty . . . as the war began.[50]

3. The most striking reports of godly intervention revolved around multiple angelic sightings by both Israeli and Arab forces. In each instance, these angels helped the Israeli army to victory. Remember, there were multiple reports from various sources and at various times. These were really angels!

4. Here is one example from the 1950s of an angelic intervention: The Israeli soldier, Gershon Salomon, a member of the IDF (Israel Defense Forces) in 1958, was involved in a battle on the Golan Heights against the Syrian Army. After Salomon was run over by an enemy tank, the Syrian soldiers advanced toward him to "finish him off." Suddenly, they ran away.

Why? At a later date, Syrian soldiers reported to United Nations officers that they had seen thousands of angels around Salomon and had, therefore, fled in haste. At the same time that the Syrians were running away, Gershon heard the voice of God speaking to him. God was not yet finished with him. In fact, he became convinced that God wanted him to devote the remainder of his life to work on the Temple Mount. Salomon became the leader of the Temple Mount Faithful organization.[51]

5. Although it was not an angelic sighting, one additional, similar, incredible sighting was confirmed by Israeli and enemy forces in both the 1948 and 1967 wars. In each of these wars, separated by nineteen years, a small squad of Israeli soldiers became pinned down by much larger, and well-armed, advancing enemy forces. In both instances, the Israeli soldiers quickly used up their remaining ammunition in a desperate attempt to defend themselves. Seemingly nothing lay between these brave soldiers and total annihilation. As the enemy soldiers approached, guns at the ready, they all suddenly stopped. Then, in complete awe and surprise, every one of these men looked up and over the heads of the Jewish soldiers. Many of them called out the name of the Jewish patriarch, Abraham. Already having stopped their advance, the enemy soldiers quickly turned and ran away. These small bands of Israeli soldiers, those in the war of Independence of 1948 and those in the famous Six-Day War of 1967, could not believe or understand what had just happened. They had been saved, miraculously, by God. They all lived to tell the story. In both cases, confirmation was provided by some of the enemy forces. They had actually seen the figure of Abraham – larger than life. God must have brought the Jewish patriarch into the scene to save the brave Israeli soldiers from certain death. The fact that this figure was

immediately identified as Abraham also had to come from a God-given miracle. For this incredible event to happen once would be fantastic; yet, it happened at least twice, separated by nineteen years, under almost identical circumstances.[52]

6. After evaluating the many reports that he heard from all combatants that he interviewed and seeing for himself the course of the Six-Day War, the military correspondent for the secular Haaretz Newspaper summed it up with the report: **"Even a non-religious person must admit this war was fought with help from heaven."**[53]

7. Col. Uri Banari gave an interesting account of the Israeli conquest of Shechem. Although the total story is more involved, the essence is that thousands of Arabs mistook advancing Israeli troops for their own allies. The Israeli army just walked in while their enemy welcomed them by waving white handkerchiefs. The enemy crowds cheered their entrance. At one point, finally, a shot was fired in the air by one of the Jewish soldiers because an Arab guard refused to disarm. The Arabs ran for cover, followed this with the raising of the white flag of surrender, and that battle was over... although it cannot really be called a battle. Later, it came out that the Arab forces there had mistaken the Israeli army for an allied Iraqi force. Once again, God's providential care came to the aid of Israel. It surely can be easy when God does the fighting.[54]

8. At one point, an Egyptian truck mounted with machine guns approached two lone soldiers, each armed only with a rifle and a few bullets. Having been caught unaware, these two young Israelis waited for the worst. They knew their time had come to die, so they aimed their guns and prepared to go down fighting. The truck stopped. No shots rang out. They slowly approached the truck. Still no shots. When they arrived at a point where they could see into the truck,

eighteen enemy soldiers were looking out at them in fear for their own lives. Quickly, the Israeli soldiers yelled out, "Hands up!" That did it. The Arabs gave up immediately. The two lone Jewish men walked the enemy men back to their base. On the way, one of them asked why the eighteen men did not simply blast away at the two Jews with their guns and/or the machine guns. Amazingly, the answer was, "I don't know. My arms froze – they became paralyzed. My whole body was paralyzed, and I don't know why." That same Israeli soldier replied later when questioned, "How can one say that God didn't help us?"[55]

9.   The Six-Day War resulted in an incredibly unlikely series of events leading up to an impressive victory for Israel. Israeli forces fought hard and courageously. However, it was so apparent to the officers at West Point that there was no way that Israel should have won that war on its own merits, that they will not even study that war in their classes concerning the tactics and strategy of war. In other words, given that an army cannot typically plan on God intervening so blatantly and frequently to bring it victory, the faculty at West Point felt it a waste of their time to study the tactics of that particular war. **One of their generals said that what concerns West Point is the study of tactics and strategy, not miracles.** That is quite a revealing statement.[56]

10. Yom Kippur War: At one point in this 1973 war, an Israeli soldier took captive a column of Egyptian soldiers (as did Sgt. York in WWI), and led them to his fellow soldiers and captivity. When asked why he allowed a lone soldier to capture his entire group of men, the Egyptian responded with surprise, "One soldier? There were thousands of them." He reported seeing all of these Jewish soldiers from a distance. As he approached, eventually all but the one Israeli soldier disappeared. However, the Egyptian column

surrendered in fear of their lives. Of course, the Israeli soldier was mystified, as he was not privy to the surrounding army of angels provided by God. God has promised that Israel will not again be defeated and lose their nation, "No harm will befall you, no disaster will come near your tent, for He will command His angels concerning you, to guard you in all your ways" (Psalm 91:10-11).

11. Yom Kippur War: Commander David Yinni, was preparing to retreat from the Syrian army, when he realized that he and his men were trapped in the middle of a minefield. He quickly ordered his men to hit the dirt and by crawling carefully, and using their bayonets, to clear the mines. They had to dig over two feet deep and then carefully disengage each encountered mine. The slightest mistake and they would be blown up. They had to finish clearing the mines in order to escape the oncoming Syrian force. The morning was approaching quickly. This was a painstaking job and it was taking far too long to finish in time. **One of his men prayed. Suddenly, a windstorm came upon them out of nowhere. It was so strong that it lifted up their tanks and rocked them.** By the time the storm moved on, it had blown off thirty inches of topsoil. That was seemingly impossible, yet it happened. The Israeli soldiers could then see every single mine, walk between them and quickly make their escape. God once again had saved His people.[57]

There are many more amazing miracles that occurred in these wars. However, hopefully, the point has been made. God definitely has His hand on Israel and will continue to protect this nation throughout these end times and into the Tribulation. Plenty of other nations will try to drive Israel into the sea, but none will succeed. Many a miracle will be sent by God, as necessary, to defend that little country of promise. It will be interesting to watch in the years to come.

30. The Ancient City of Petra Will Exist and Become the Refuge for Fleeing Jews (from the Forces of the Antichrist) During the Great Tribulation:

> "I will surely gather all of you, O Jacob; I will surely bring together the remnant of Israel. I will bring them together like *sheep in a pen*, like a flock in its pasture; the place will throng with people." (Micah 2:12) "Sheep in a pen" in Hebrew is the name for the city of Bozrah. Today, what remains of that ancient city is the city of Petra, located in southern Jordan.

> "So when you see standing in the holy place 'the abomination that causes desolation,' spoken of through the prophet Daniel--let the reader understand-- then let those who are in Judea flee to the mountains." (Matt 24:15-16)

The mountains spoken of here by Jesus include the mountains of Petra. Petra is the greatest tourist attraction in Jordan. It is simply a beautiful collection of awe-inspiring mountains that are a beautiful rose red color. Vast numbers of carved out caves, buildings, streets and tombs can be seen all over the landscape. This city is a monument to the industriousness of the ancient Nabataeans who lived and developed this mountainous desert terrain between the sixth century B.C. until they were absorbed into the Roman Empire at the end of the first century A.D.

In the vision that John received while on the Isle of Patmos, he saw the Israelites, who had turned to Jesus during the Tribulation, escape into the area surrounding Jerusalem. This was the only way that they could avoid the wrath of the Antichrist. Many died a martyr's death because of their faithful allegiance to their Messiah.

Others were able to run and hide in places such as Petra. "The woman fled into the desert to a place prepared for her by God, where she might be taken care of for **1,260 days**." (Rev 12:6)

In 1994, a treaty was signed between Israel and Jordan. Jordan joined Egypt as only the second Arab nation to normalize relations with Israel. Since that time, there has been a resurgence of travel into that ancient and beautiful "rock" city of Petra. Following the agreements, Israel and Jordan opened their borders. Several border crossings were erected, allowing tourists, merchants and workers to travel between the two countries. Israeli tourists frequently visit Jordan, many to see the "Red Rock" of Petra. Many tourist trips to Israel that originate in the United States include Petra as one of their stops.

Given this recent normalization of relations between Israel and Jordan, it will make it much easier for the frightened Jews of the Tribulation to flee to their old standby Petra. It is an excellent hiding place southeast of Jerusalem that is filled with carved out mountains all ready to use as living quarters as they wait for the coming of the Messiah during the final 3 ½ years of the seven year Tribulation. The 1994 treaty may be just one more evidence of God's providential care in this world to prepare for the Second Coming of His Son, Jesus. Because of this treaty and the resultant increased tourist travel to Petra, people in Jerusalem are markedly more aware of that area and the refuge it will have to offer during the coming terrible days of tribulation.

31. God Will Provide Birds of Prey and Wild Animals to Clean Up the Dead:

The apocalyptic books of the Bible reference many wars that will arise just prior to the coming of the Lord. Ezekiel (chapters 38 and 39) wrote concerning a war that will precede Armageddon and wreck terrible damage and death upon the forces that invade Israel. Asaph, the Psalmist, also wrote of another fierce war that would result in much death and destruction (i.e., Psalm 83). Certainly, the war that will result in more death than all others will be the war of Armageddon. Due to the combination of massive manpower, powerful armaments and, most likely, nuclear destruction, millions of people will die on the battlefields of Israel. As God will be supernaturally protecting Israel, most of the dead will be enemy combatants. God wrote long ago of one method that He planned to use to clean up the battlefields…

> And I saw an angel standing in the sun, who cried in a loud voice to all the birds flying in midair, "Come, gather together for the great supper of God,[18] so that **you may eat the flesh of kings, generals, and mighty men, of horses and their riders, and the flesh of all people, free and slave, small and great.**"[19] Then I saw the beast and the kings of the earth and their armies gathered together to make war against the rider on the horse and his army.[20] But the beast was captured, and with him the false prophet who had performed the miraculous signs on his behalf. With these signs he had deluded those who had received the mark of the beast and worshiped his image. The two of them were thrown alive into the fiery lake of burning sulfur.[21] The rest of them were killed with the sword that came out of the mouth of the rider on the horse, and **all the birds gorged themselves on their flesh**. (Rev 19:17-21)

> On the mountains of Israel you [Gog, present day Russia] will fall, you and all your troops and the nations with you. I will give you as food to all kinds of carrion birds and to the wild animals. (Ezek 39:4)

> "Son of man, this is what the Sovereign LORD says: **Call out to every kind of bird and all the wild animals: 'Assemble and come together from all around to the sacrifice I am preparing for you, the great sacrifice on**

the mountains of Israel. **There you will eat flesh and drink blood.** [18] **You will eat the flesh of mighty men and drink the blood of the princes of the earth as if they were rams and lambs, goats and bulls--all of them fattened animals from Bashan.'"...** [21] "I will display my glory among the nations, and all the nations will see the punishment I inflict and the hand I lay upon them.[22] **From that day forward the house of Israel will know that I am the Lord their God."** (Ezek 39:17-18,21-22)

The Lord is angry with all nations; his wrath is upon all their armies. He will totally destroy them, he will give them over to slaughter. For **the Lord has a sacrifice in Bozrah and a great slaughter in Edom.** [7] And the wild oxen will fall with them, the bull calves and the great bulls. Their land will be drenched with blood, and the dust will be soaked with fat. [8] For the LORD has a day of vengeance, a year of retribution, to uphold Zion's cause... [11] **The desert owl and screech owl will possess it; the great owl and the raven will nest there.** God will stretch out over Edom the measuring line of chaos and the plumb line of desolation... [13] **Thorns will overrun her citadels, nettles and brambles her strongholds. She will become a haunt for jackals, a home for owls.** [14] **Desert creatures will meet with hyenas, and wild goats will bleat to each other;** there the night creatures will also repose and find for themselves places of rest. (Isaiah 34:2,6-8,11,13-14)

In the verses from Revelation, Ezekiel, and Isaiah listed above, God is warning the nations that will come against Israel in the last days that it will not end well for them. In fact, millions of Israel's enemies will die in the battle of Armageddon which will take place at Megiddo. Jesus Christ Himself will defeat the forces of Satan at that time. As noted above, many more will die in the battles described in Ezekiel 38/39 and Psalm 83. What preparations might God be making for these battlefields now? One should keep in mind that there probably will be a significant component of nuclear debris that will make this clean-up process very difficult and dangerous.

There must be massive quantities of birds of prey in order to accomplish the cleaning up of the dead on that vast battlefield... at least in the manner God sees fit to "clean it up." That, in turn, brings us to the point of this "sign." Interestingly, the plains of Megiddo have the greatest population of this kind of bird in the entire world. Number one in the world! A coincidence? Maybe... but probably not. Up to one billion birds of this type fly over Israel each spring. One to four billion migratory birds, many being raptors-carrion (eaters of dead flesh) fly over the land of Israel in the fall. Thirty-four species of these man-eating birds of prey visit or live in the area of Megiddo. Israel has turned this area into a preserve for these birds of prey, and they are flourishing. Tiny Israel is a land bridge; because Israel is connected to Egypt, birds don't have to make the difficult journey over the Mediterranean. They fly by way of Israel. Some stop off and remain in Israel living in the preserves that have been set up in recent decades. These birds are apparently readying themselves for the enormous feast to come.

Along with the numerous birds of prey in the area of Megiddo, there are significant numbers of these birds and wild desert animals in the Petra and Bozrah region just below the Dead Sea as well. This area will be where many of the enemies of Israel fall in battle during the earlier wars of the Tribulation. The bottom line is that God in His providence has provided for an amazing quantity of *birds of prey* and *scavenger animals* in the exact areas that the Bible foretells will one day be filled with fallen enemy forces. After the war detailed in Ezekiel, it will take seven years for the clean-up to be completed... probably taking so long due to the utmost care that will be required after nuclear contamination. These birds and animals will be useful in this gruesome, yet necessary, activity.

Summation of Prophecies Related to the Nation and People of Israel:

God gave the world many signs to herald the Second Coming of His Son, the Messiah. These signs are found throughout the Old and the New Testaments. As previously explained, the Rapture will be the glorious event that leads ultimately to the return of Jesus to this earth. His Second Coming will see Jesus descend triumphantly onto the Mount of Olives accompanied by His saints. He will then quickly defeat the forces of evil and usher in the Millennial Kingdom. In recent decades, dozens of these signs have come to fruition, *especially those signs that concern the chosen people,* Israel and the Jews.

In May, 1948, Israel became a nation once again. It had been two thousand years since the Jewish people had a land to call their home. This was an unprecedented event. Nothing like this has ever happened to any other nation in world history. For the first time since just after the death of Solomon, Israel was a unified nation; Jews from every tribe returned from all over the globe. For some, this was not very difficult, but for others, many obstacles needed to be overcome. The national language of Hebrew was reborn – a remarkable achievement. As one important result of the Six-Day War of 1967, Jerusalem became the Israeli capital once again. Intriguingly, even the rebuilding of this city has followed the course prophesied in the Old Testament. Each of these events was the absolute fulfillment of prophecy.

In the Old Testament, God foretold of the days when He would once again bless Israel after bringing the Jews back into their land. God said these blessings would manifest in many ways: increased water in the land would change the deserts to lush vineyards, orchards, and forests. This has come to pass. Excellent quantity and quality of flowers and vegetables have been a great blessing to the people. God said that in the latter days, great natural resources would be discovered in the land and under the sea. They certainly have been. Amazing quantities have been discovered just within the past five years.

The prophets also wrote of the Third Temple being desecrated halfway through the seven year Tribulation. Given all of the other signs currently noted to be present, it should not be surprising that everything needed for the rebuilding of this Temple is now ready. The architectural plans are complete. The Levitical priests have been chosen, outfitted and have been well trained. The instruments of worship have been constructed and are ready for use. The oil of anointing, the required "perfect" red heifer, and all other things required for Temple worship are now ready and waiting for the Messiah's return. Possibly the only question left may relate to the Ark of the Covenant. Many are convinced that its whereabouts is already known. Even if this is not the case, God will reveal its location when the time for Temple worship arrives. All of these other things have already come to pass in just the last several decades.

God also warned that Israel and its capital city, Jerusalem, would be fought over by other nations in the last days. It would be a land divided. Eventually, this would lead to war. Due to the situation in the Middle East, many nations of the world are already on the precipice of war against Israel – unfortunately, the next war has the distinct possibility of being a nuclear war of mammoth proportions. The Bible tells us that this scenario will exist just prior to the world moving into the Tribulation.

God also told of a future day when Russia would ally with Iran and some of Iran's neighbors to invade Israel. This war is on the horizon even now. Russia and Iran have recently become quite the pair of trading partners. Iran's interest revolves around its obtaining nuclear weapons technology – again pointing to the coming destruction. Other wars have also been prophesied in the Old Testament and we can see these future events begin to unfold as we look at the 200 million man army of Communist China, and the current capability for the drying up of the Euphrates River – all are further fulfillment of end-time prophecies.

Although the Bible does say that Israel will be involved in wars in these last days, it also points out that they will be under the supernatural protection of God. They will not be defeated in battle. There are dozens of incredible examples that show the truth of this fantastic prophecy.

Israel will not be led by a king in these latter days. Not until the Messiah returns will it be a monarchy again. However, Israel will resist turning to this Messiah, King, until the Tribulation. During that seven year period of time, the majority of the Jews will finally recognize Jesus as the true Messiah. As Paul wrote under the direction of the Holy Spirit, "Israel has experienced a hardening in part until the full number of the Gentiles has come in. 26 And so all Israel will be saved" (Romans 11:25-26). In fact, Jesus will come at the conclusion of the Tribulation, walk through the currently sealed Eastern Gate, and rescue Israel during the battle of Armageddon. Far more importantly, Jesus will save them eternally after they turn to Him in faith as the true sacrificial Lamb of God. So, as we have seen, God has already given the world many signs of His Son's soon return. In fact, He has given us even more; they will be presented in the next two sections of this book.

Figure 9: Petra – Mountains replete with caves in which to hide

Figure 10: Megiddo – Scene of the Battle of Armageddon

Section 2:

THE WORLD IN THE LATTER DAYS

I T IS TRUE that the majority of the end-time signs concern the people and nation of Israel in some manner. However, God has also given an overview of what the world, as a whole, will be like in the years leading up to the Second Coming. He did this through several of the Old Testament prophets and, as will be seen in Section 3, God revealed much about the state of the world in the latter days through the preaching of His Son.

In this section, prophecies given to the prophet Daniel and the Apostle John concerning the end-time political, economic, and military systems of the world will be reviewed. According to Bible prophecy, there will be a revival of the old Roman Empire as the end time approaches. This revived empire will coincide with a concerted effort by many of the great leaders of the world to effect a one world government. Interestingly, this one world government will one day be led by a charismatic and powerful leader of the aforementioned revived Roman Empire. The details of these events will be given in the next chapter.

One additional major topic revealed in biblical eschatology concerns the incredible scientific advancements that will be seen in the latter days. The various technological capabilities required to fulfill certain end-time biblical prophecies could not possibly have been imagined when they were written down by the prophets. It is only in this generation that people are able to understand the specific technologies described suggested over two thousand years ago. Yet, the Bible did say that the world would have these capabilities just prior to the Second Coming. It does have them now. Many examples of these breakthroughs are discussed in chapter 8.

The prophet Joel was given one additional prophecy of the end times that proves to be extremely interesting. Joel was shown that God planned to unveil a very incredible spiritual blessing on all mankind after Israel was back in their land, after they had begun to receive their many promised blessings from God. God told Joel that "afterward, I will pour out my Spirit on all people" (Joel 2:28). The last sign discussed in this section will reveal the amazing truth of this promise now being experienced by tens of thousands of people in the Middle East.

Keep in mind, the signs that God has given to our generation. They include the emergence of a revived Roman Empire, the inexorable path that appears to be taking the nations of the world toward a one world government and economic system, phenomenal scientific advancements that have been made in recent history, and the amazing spiritual outpouring we are seeing today in the Middle East. None of these were ever seen prior to these past few decades. This, of course, is the same situation as was noted with the signs relating to Israel and the end times. The conclusion also must be the same… we should recognize that the Rapture must be coming soon.

Chapter 7

THERE WILL BE A WORLDWIDE POLITICAL AND ECONOMIC SYSTEM IN THE LAST DAYS

THE PROPHET DANIEL was given a vision of a succession of world empires beginning with the Babylonian Empire led by King Nebuchadnezzar. God also revealed that the world empire existing at the time of the Second Coming of the Messiah would include, in some manner, a revival of the nations that had once formed the Roman Empire. The Antichrist will be introduced to the world as its new, charismatic, and very powerful leader, probably very soon after the Rapture.

The city of Babylon will also be rebuilt and assume a leadership role economically during the Tribulation in this final world governmental system. Although Babylon will once again be an important city for a short season, God will destroy it as the Tribulation draws to a close.

There is a great deal of evidence that various world leaders have been pursuing a one world government for almost a century. It is also interesting to note how much effort and money has been expended in a concerted project to rebuild the city of Babylon in the last several years. Many additional details follow in the signs noted below.

32. Revival of Roman Empire:

The Bible says that in the latter days the Roman Empire will revive, become powerful, and then be quickly and decisively defeated by the coming of the Lord Jesus. Details of how this will occur were given to a young Jewish man, over 2,500 years ago. The story is found in the Old Testament book of Daniel. King Nebuchadnezzar of Babylon was very troubled by a recurring dream sent to him by God. He was desperate to understand its meaning. None of his wise men were able to provide him with the answers he sought. Finally, a young Israelite, Daniel, came forward and said that his God would reveal the mystery. The King listened intently as Daniel first described the dream the king had received, and then gave the interpretation...

> "You looked, O king, and there before you stood a large statue--an enormous, dazzling statue, awesome in appearance.[32] The **head of the statue was made of pure gold**, its **chest and arms of silver**, its **belly and thighs of bronze**,[33] **its legs of iron, its feet partly of iron and partly of baked clay.**[34] **While you were watching, a rock was cut out, but *not by human hands*. It struck the statue on its feet of iron and clay and smashed them.**[35] **Then the iron, the clay, the bronze, the silver and the gold were broken to pieces** at the same time and became like chaff on a threshing floor in the summer. The wind swept them away without leaving a trace. But the rock that struck the statue became a huge mountain and filled the whole earth. This was the dream, and **now we will interpret it to the king.**[37] You, O king, are the king of kings. The God of heaven has given you dominion and power and might and glory;[38] in your hands he has placed mankind and the beasts of the field and the birds of the air. Wherever they live, he has made you ruler over them all. **You are that head of gold.**[39] After you, another kingdom will rise, inferior to yours. Next, a third kingdom, one of bronze,

will rule over the whole earth.[40] Finally, there will be a **fourth kingdom, strong as iron**--for iron breaks and smashes everything--and as iron breaks things to pieces, so it will crush and break all the others.[41] Just as you saw that **the feet and toes were partly of baked clay and partly of iron, so this will be a divided kingdom; yet it will have some of the strength of iron in it, even as you saw iron mixed with clay.**[42] **As the toes were partly iron and partly clay, so this kingdom will be partly strong and partly brittle.**[43] **And just as you saw the iron mixed with baked clay, so the people will be a mixture and will not remain united, any more than iron mixes with clay."** (Dan 2:31-43)

Prior to the Roman Empire coming into power, there were three other kingdoms that had conquered and ruled the Middle Eastern world, including Israel and the holy city of Jerusalem. The first three kingdoms were Babylonia, Medo-Persia, and Greece. These three identities are confirmed in subsequent chapters of Daniel. The fourth world kingdom to come onto the scene was to be the Roman Empire. This was represented by the legs of iron. The two iron legs indicate that this was to be a very powerful empire that would have two divisions. Daniel was told by God that it would eventually become divided into ten parts (represented by the ten toes of a mixture of clay and iron). When in this form, it will be a mixture of strong and weak parts (e.g., these could be ten nations or ten divisions of a larger entity) and, ultimately, will not stay united. As God will reveal in chapter 7 and in the book of The Revelation, there will come a time when Jesus Himself will come to earth to defeat this federation just before He sets up His Millennial Kingdom on earth. Chapter 7 also goes into more detail on this same topic after Daniel received another similar vision. This vision added some additional information on the leadership of this revived kingdom.

Daniel said: "In my vision at night I looked, and there before me were the four winds of heaven churning up the great sea.³ Four great beasts, each different from the others, came up out of the sea. ⁴ "The **first was like a lion**, and it had the wings of an eagle. I watched until its wings were torn off and it was lifted from the ground so that it stood on two feet like a man, and the heart of a man was given to it. ⁵ And there before me was **a second beast, which looked like a bear**. It was raised up on one of its sides, and it had three ribs in its mouth between its teeth. It was told, 'Get up and eat your fill of flesh!'⁶ After that, I looked, and there before me was another beast, **one that looked like a leopard**. And on its back it had four wings like those of a bird. This beast had four heads, and it was given authority to rule.⁷ After that, in my vision at night I looked, and there before me was **a fourth beast--terrifying and frightening and very powerful**. It had large iron teeth; it crushed and devoured its victims and trampled underfoot whatever was left. **It was different from all the former beasts, and it had ten horns.**⁸ While I was thinking about the horns, **there before me was another horn, a little one, which came up among them; and three of the first horns were uprooted before it. This horn had eyes like the eyes of a man and a mouth that spoke boastfully."** Dan 7:2-8

We see that in verse 7 and 8 above, that the final form of the Roman Empire will have one individual (a little horn) which will rise up to uproot three of the original ten horns (i.e., there will be ten "divisions" of the kingdom in the latter days) and take over as leader. The word "horn" in the Bible, when used in this context, always represents an individual with power. Note that the Bible shows that this "horn" will have the characteristics of a man... in fact, he will be a man, the Antichrist. This "Little Horn" will take on the whole world for a time and be very successful for a season. In fact, the Antichrist will be the most powerful figure in the world throughout the seven year Tribulation. He will eventually wage war against Christians (the saints). Ultimately, the Messiah will return to earth to defeat this Antichrist in the terrible battle of Armageddon, followed by the setting up His Millennial Kingdom. This is pointed out in the last few verses of Daniel 7.

> As I watched, **this horn was waging war against the saints and defeating them,** [22] **until the Ancient of Days came and pronounced judgment in favor of the saints of the Most High, and the time came when they possessed the kingdom.**[23] He gave me this explanation: "The fourth beast is a fourth kingdom that will appear on earth. It will be different from all the other kingdoms and will devour the whole earth, trampling it down and crushing it. [24] The ten horns are ten kings who will come from this kingdom. After them another king will arise, different from the earlier ones; he will subdue three kings ... [25] He will speak against the Most High and oppress his saints and try to change the set times and the laws. The saints will be handed over to him for a time, times and half a time.[26] But the court will sit, and **his power will be taken away and completely destroyed forever.**[27] Then the sovereignty, power and greatness of the kingdoms under the whole heaven will be handed over to the saints, the people of the Most High. His kingdom will be an everlasting kingdom, and all rulers will worship and obey him." (Dan 7:21-27)

In summary, the Book of Daniel, in chapters 2 and 7, carefully outlines the description by the prophet Daniel of a very important dream of King Nebuchadnezzar and one additional vision that God gave to Daniel. Both of these miraculous events resulted in amazing prophecies concerning the various world powers that would extend over several thousand years of world history. The book of Daniel foretold the fact that at some point in the future, the fourth world power, the Roman Empire, would reconstitute and be ruled by one very powerful Anti-Christian leader... the Antichrist.

It is the opinion of every prophecy scholar that holds to the premillennial tribulation view, that the fourth kingdom, the Roman Empire, will be reborn in the latter days. The dream of Nebuchadnezzar and Daniel's own vision is interpreted as follows:

1. The first kingdom – (head of fine gold = the **lion**) --- represents Babylon
2. The second kingdom – (chest and arms of silver = **bear**) --- represents the Medes and Persians; Medo-Persia
3. The third kingdom – (thighs of bronze = **leopard**) --- represents Greece and their various leaders
4. The fourth kingdom – (legs of iron = **beast**) --- represents Rome

   The *fourth kingdom revived* --- represents the Roman Empire revived with ten divisions, eventually giving its power to a very charismatic world leader, the Antichrist (the idea of a charismatic world leader wielding great power is not that unusual in history... note how Adolph Hitler rapidly rose to power in Nazi Germany)

The fourth kingdom is described as having two legs. As mentioned earlier, these two legs represent the two divisions of the Roman Empire. Rome was divided for centuries into western and eastern divisions – the West had its capital in Rome, the East had its capital in Istanbul. The western portion of the empire fell apart in A.D. 476. The eastern portion, the Byzantine Empire, lasted until A.D. 1453.

Eventually, these two iron legs will "grow" into ten toes, being a mixture of iron and clay – a mixture of strong and weak. In these latter days, since the nation of Israel has been re-established, there has been evidence of the coming together of the many nations of the old Roman Empire. We know that there has to be a revival of the Roman Empire because the first one never had a ten nation confederacy, it certainly was never suddenly crushed by the Messiah, and it obviously was not present on the earth at Christ's Second Coming... as that has yet to occur.

The important question to be asked is what, if any, evidence is there that the Roman Empire is beginning to come back into power? For so many centuries, it has been non-existent.

Although there have been attempts by leaders such as Napoleon and Hitler to take over Europe forcibly, never has there been anything in world history that could be mistaken for a revival of the old Roman Empire. Given that the Antichrist will be the leader of the revived Roman Empire, and that he will assume his world leadership role very soon after the Rapture, we would expect to see at least some signs of a revival of this empire if we are living in the latter days. As it turns out, we do see these signs today.

Let's take a look at what has been going on over the last half-century. Of course, we know that Israel became a nation once again in 1948. Jerusalem became part of Israel in 1967. The clock began ticking with these events. David Jeremiah noted in his recent book, *What In The World Is Going On*, that Winston Churchill said the path to European peace and prosperity required that, "We must build a United States of Europe."[1] Leaders of the European nations realized that they had to unite to avoid a repeat of the two World Wars they had suffered through during the previous half century. Not only that, but they knew that individually their countries could not compete with the United States and the Soviet Union. China would also one day be a major competitor. Most agreed with Churchill, a united Europe was needed. They would unite to pool their physical and intellectual resources. Together they would be able to compete on the international stage.

After several smaller steps towards this reunification, on March 25, 1957, the Treaty of Rome was signed by six European nations to create the European Economic Community – the Common Market.

These nations were France, Belgium, Germany, Italy, Netherlands, and Luxembourg. Interestingly, and possibly providentially, this treaty was signed in Rome. The United Kingdom, Ireland, and Denmark joined in 1973; Greece was added in 1981, and Portugal and Spain joined in 1986. This added up to twelve nations at that time. The Berlin Wall fell in 1989 and resulted in East Germany becoming a member nation as it combined with West Germany, already a member. Then, in 1991, the Soviet Union dissolved into its various member nations. Austria, Finland, and Sweden became members in 1995. The inexorable march toward unification continued on May 1, 2004, when ten additional nations signed on. The total expanded to its current total of twenty-seven in 2007 with the addition of Romania and Bulgaria. With all of these additions, there are now over 500,000 million people in the EU. In 2007, the U.S. lost its seat to the European Union (EU) as the world's largest economy. In 2011, the EU's economy produced $15.4 trillion in goods and services, while the U.S. GDP came in second at $15.0 trillion. Euro coins and banknotes were introduced into circulation in the world markets on January 1, 2002. It is already competing with the dollar internationally. "The EU now has an economy of scale that eats into the comparative advantage the U.S. has traditionally enjoyed. Furthermore, the EU's currency, the euro, is now competing with the dollar as a global currency. Thanks to these competitive pressures, a U.S. recession could be the precursor to a lower standard of living that may not return to previous, stronger levels."[2]

The Treaty of Lisbon, which went into effect on December 1, 2009, established a term of 2½ years for the office of President of the European Council. Herman Van Rompuy of Belgium was the first man elected to this important position. Jose Manuel Barroso is currently the President of the European Commission, also a position of leadership in the EU. He is serving his second five year term. There is no one in the EU who has taken a firm role as the overall leader of that organization... yet. In fact, the power structure within the EU is not very well defined. Even the specific duties of each of the presidents are debatable. However, one day in the future, the Bible tells us that one man will ascend to ultimate power. The organization required for the biblical Antichrist to come onto the scene is now in place.

As is quite obvious, over the past fifty years there has been a very impressive amalgamation of the nations that represent those countries and lands that used to make up the old Roman Empire. In other words, we have seen the *revival of the old Roman Empire*. The European Union is now very large and wields much power, especially economic power.

However, just as Daniel's prophecy foretold, this current "empire" (i.e., the European Union) does appear to be a combination of iron and clay. The EU has much power economically, politically, and even militarily, but there are problems with several weak member states, and significant racial, cultural, and religious tensions within the union. Greece, for example, has recently been rescued out of bankruptcy on multiple occasions. Spain and Ireland are also struggling financially. Not only are there serious economic issues, but there is a significant amount of tension between Muslims and Christians within many of these nation-states.

Most prophecy scholars believe that the world is on the precipice of a coming world government that will be ruled by one very impressive, charismatic man coming out of this European Union… the future Antichrist. Almost assuredly, a worldwide economic and geopolitical crisis will be the impetus for this to happen. Prior to this occurring, the European Union will be restructured in some fashion to contain ten divisions. In fact, there have already been discussions of doing this among the member nations of the union. Out of this conglomerate of nations will come the Antichrist. He will at first be welcomed as the answer to the world's growing problems. He will bring temporary peace to Israel and the world. But then, literally, all of hell's demons will break loose and bring great destruction onto

Jerusalem, Israel and new believers in Christ. A showdown will come as the end of the Great Tribulation is approached.

The point to remember is that there is significant evidence showing that the European nations have already come together in great numbers (twenty-seven nations) to form what could – for the purposes of understanding Bible prophecy - be reasonably referred to as the nascent form of the revived Roman Empire. This is just one more reason to believe that we are living in the latter days.

33. One World Government:

> He was given power to make war against the saints and to conquer them. And **he was given authority over every tribe, people, language and nation.**[8] All inhabitants of the earth will worship the beast--all whose names have not been written in the book of life belonging to the Lamb that was slain from the creation of the world. (Rev 13:7-8)

According to the Bible, in the last days the world will be governed by one central government. At that time, all people will come under the leadership and the control of one person... the leader of that world government. This will be a New World Order. The Bible refers to the ultimate and final world leader as the Antichrist. At first, he will be looked upon as a very charismatic and very competent leader. He will be asked to step into this powerful role because of his obvious ability to bring the world together. Almost assuredly, the nations of the world will have been undergoing a time of marked unrest... if not chaos. This Antichrist will be capable of uniting the nations who had previously been at enmity with one another.

Interestingly, even in the 1960s the idea of a New World Order was broached in some of the speeches and writings of very impressive world leaders. On January 17, 1961, in a portion of his farewell address, President Dwight Eisenhower warned the people of the

United States to always be alert to the possibility of losing their freedom. He said, "The potential for the disastrous rise of misplaced power exists and will persist."[3] President Kennedy also warned of the threat of losing our freedom to powerful, yet, secretive enemies. While President he once stated that, "We are opposed around the world by a monolithic and ruthless conspiracy that relies primarily on covert means for expanding its sphere of influence."[4] However, in general, during those years the idea of a New World Order was considered by most people to be more of a conspiracy theory by certain evangelical Christians who viewed it as a lead-in to the end times. Therefore, it may be worthwhile to take a brief look at what has been taking place throughout the world over the last century that has prepared the way for this New World Order.

For almost fifty years, prophecy scholars have suggested that there are several powerful, yet secretive, societies in the world who have as one of their goals the eventual formation of a global government. Grant Jeffrey wrote extensively on this subject in his book, *Final Warning*. His premise was that "at the turn of the century the secret powers who truly control world events from behind the scenes began to create organizations to assure their ability to dominate future world events and ultimately produce the one-world government they desired."[5] These men felt that with time and careful planning, very powerful and influential world organizations, working together in a crisis situation, would be able to create a global government over which they exerted ultimate control. They realized that it would likely take several generations to bring this idea to its final realization. However, they would still be able to wield great power and influence while working toward this goal. The first step of this process is considered to be the U.S. Federal Reserve Banking System, formed in 1913. For the first time in the history of the United States, the control of the U.S. economy and banking system was removed in large part from the Congress and passed on to this powerful private organization. It remains there to this day. Only eight years later, the next aspect of this worldwide group of organizations was convened. In 1921, the Council on Foreign Relations (CFR) was established. Ostensibly this group was created to "advise their respective governments on economic policy and international relations."[6] However, several members of this organization have told of a deeper, underlying purpose of the CFR. For example, Carroll Quigley, a mentor of President Clinton, said, "The CFR is the American Branch of a society which originated in England, and which believes that national boundaries should be obliterated, and a one-world rule established."[7] Another former respected member of the CFR, Rear Admiral Chester Ward, warned the American people of the organization's intentions when he stated, "The most powerful clique in these elitist groups have one objective in common – they want to bring about the surrender of the national sovereignty of the national independence of the United States."[8] Dan Smoot, a former FBI staff member, concurred when he said, "The ultimate aim of the CFR is to create a one-world socialist system, and to make the U.S. an official part of it."[9] Saul Mendlovitz, the founding director of the World Order Models Project, once noted, "As we have already shown and will further demonstrate, the CFR and its influential members are also on record favoring and promoting world government. However, most of these public CFR utterances have appeared in publications and speeches intended for a select, sympathetic audience where the new world order adepts can 'unblushingly' (in the words of Lincoln Bloomfield) contemplate and discuss 'world government.'"[10] The above quotes are but a few of dozens that could be cited showing the long-range goals of the Council on Foreign Relations.

There have been other organizations that have been created with the same basic goals of the CFR. Soon after WWII, the United Nations was formed. Over 70% of the U.S. planning committee for the U.N. were CFR members. In 1973, the Trilateral Commission was created. Jimmy Carter, David Rockefeller and Zbigniew

Brzezinski were founding members of this group. Many of the members of the CFR are also now members of this commission. In 1979, the Manchester Union Leader ran an editorial during that presidential primary season warning the people that, "It is quite clear that this group of extremely powerful men is out to rule the world."[11] Since the Carter administration many, if not most, of the positions in every administration have been filled by men who belong to the CFR and/or the Trilateral Commission.

In addition to the aforementioned organizations, others with the same goals have been formed by powerful men with ambitious ideas. The most influential of these include: the Bilderbergers, the Council of Europe, the Club of Rome, and the World Federalist Movement. Virtually every nation now is governed by individuals who belong to one or more of these globalist associations.

In summary, there is no doubt that the rich and powerful of the world have worked to influence the policies and direction of their respective governments in recent history. They have accomplished this via:

- Creating several similar organizations throughout the past 100 years whereby these individuals do indeed influence many different governments on a variety of different policy issues.
- Working effectively to grow these organizations in every decade to the point where they wield vast power in the governments of most nations today.
- Once it was thought to be only the folly of conspiracy theorists to suggest that these people had an agenda to one day move the world into a New World Order whereby the nations of the world would surrender much of their sovereignty to a global governing board or individual. However, as will be pointed out in the following paragraphs, now the most

influential of these people proudly tell of their hopes and plans for this very same New World Order.

Before proceeding, it is important to point out that the vast majority of the individuals belonging to these organizations do not have any particular nefarious objectives. It is just that their world view is that mankind can and will one day be able to move our world into a New Age of enlightenment. This, they believe, will require a New World Order in order to bring to a halt the constant wars, economic crashes, worldwide famine, political infighting, etc. Those that do not believe that Jesus Christ is the ultimate answer for all of these problems instead put their faith in man.

Therefore, no longer is the idea of a New World Order an idea of only the fringe... i.e., of the so-called "crackpot" Christians. Today and for some time now, there have been many noteworthy and well-respected people who have proposed this form of government for the world.

For example, George H. W. Bush spoke about it during his term in office. On January 29, 1991, he told the nation in his State of the Union message, "What is at stake is more than one small country, it is a big idea - a **New World Order**, where diverse nations are drawn together in a common cause, to achieve the universal aspirations of mankind: peace and security, freedom, and the rule of law. Such a world is worthy of our struggle, and worthy of our children's future. Hence, we can see a new world coming into view. A world in which there is the very real prospect of a new world order. In the words of Winston Churchill, a 'world order' in which 'the principles of justice and fair play . . . protect the weak against the strong. A world where the United Nations, freed from cold war stalemate, is poised to fulfill the historic vision of its founders. A world in which freedom and respect for human rights find a home among all nations. A world in which there is the very real prospect of a new world order."[12]

A few years later while speaking at the Kennedy Center on Sept. 6, 2006, former President Bill Clinton agreed with the aforementioned comments of his predecessor, President Bush, on the New World Order. He then added "I think it is important that every American have a world view." The most admired anchorman in television history, Walter Cronkite, wrote in 1996, "if we are to avoid catastrophe, a system of world order--preferably a system of world government --is mandatory. The proud nations someday will... yield up their precious sovereignty."[13] Three years later, he received the Norman Cousins Global Governance Award at a World Federalist Association event in New York. In his acceptance speech, he said, "It seems to many of us that if we are to avoid the eventual catastrophic world conflict, **we must strengthen the United Nations as a first step toward a world government** patterned after our own government with a legislature, executive and judiciary, and police to enforce its international laws and keep the peace. To do that, of course, **we Americans will have to yield up some of our sovereignty.** That would be a bitter pill. It would take a lot of courage, a lot of faith in the new order."[14] Hillary Clinton was there to introduce Cronkite and to hail him for "inspiring us all to build a more peaceful and just world."[15]

President Obama has also spoken about this future world order as well. In fact, there are current world leaders who would like to see him in the role of the leader. Former Secretary of State, Henry Kissinger, during an interview in 2007, said that in the next four years we will see "the beginning of a New International Order." In this same interview, he said that "there was a need for a New World Order." When asked to explain the concept and purpose of this New Order, Kissinger noted, "There are so many problems in the world that can only be dealt with on a global basis." He followed this by mentioning the problems of the environment, nuclear proliferation, and energy. When asked in an interview on CNBC to give his opinion on the issue that would define the Obama administration, he answered, "He can give a new impetus to American foreign policy partly because the perception of him is so extraordinary around the world. I think his task will be to develop an overall strategy for America in this period when really a New World Order can be created. It is a great opportunity." He added that the world's current economic crisis was an opportunity to do that very thing.[16]

Gordon Brown, former Prime Minister of Britain, is also a great proponent of the New World Order. In April, 2009 he said, "This is a collective action of people working around the world working at their best. The new world order is emerging, and with it, the foundations of a new and progressive era of international cooperation."[17] European Union president, Herman Van Rompuy stated, at a Brussels' press conference, that "2009 is also the first year of global governance, with the establishment of the G-20 in the middle of the financial crisis. The climate conference in Copenhagen is another step towards the global management of our planet."[18]

The point of all of these quotes is to show just how much the idea of a New World Order has captured the imagination of the top world leaders. They want it, and they are working toward it every day.

So what would be the end result of this New World Order? It would consist of a world central bank, one global currency, and world energy control. Several people have already pointed out that a crisis (economic or military or political) would very likely be the final catalyst for bringing this New World Order into existence. For example, Henry Morgenthau, a member of the Council on Foreign Relations and treasury secretary under President Franklin D. Roosevelt, stated that "We can hardly expect the nation-state to make itself superfluous, at least not overnight. Rather, what we must aim for is recognition in the minds of all responsible statesmen that they are really nothing more than caretakers of a bankrupt international machine which will have to be transformed into a new one.[19] The key ingredient to this formula is to "financially bankrupt the international machine."[20] Grant Jeffrey suggested, "Nations will be forced to turn to the International Monetary Fund (IMF) and World Bank for a financial bailout, but only under the condition that borrowers abandon their national sovereignty."[21] Many of the world's nations are at the very brink of doing this.

In recent years, there has been much activity in the United Nations to chip away at national sovereignty. Recommendations have been made to assess a sales charge on all arms deals, international trade, international money transfers, international air and sea travel. There are those who have proposed an international income tax on all the people in the world. Now, these are only suggestions by certain U.N. organizations. In the future, these things may actually be implemented.

Some see the future of the United Nations moving toward a system like that of the European Union. Unfortunately, if that were to occur, our current capability to have a reasonable say in our national government would suffer greatly. The people of Europe have little to do with the running of the EU. The European Parliament has no significant power when compared to the *unelected* European Commission. This commission is made up of twenty-one selected (not elected) individuals. That is also where the power lies. Once a nation has lost its sovereignty, for whatever reason, they are not likely to get it back. The future New World Order will invest its power, almost assuredly, in the hands of an unelected group of people or one charismatic individual. The Bible tells us that at some time in the future, the entire world will be under the control of one man… the Antichrist. This is also consistent with where our leaders want to take us… although they have no plans to put the actual Antichrist in control. It will just work out that way.

It is an interesting fact that President George W. Bush in 2005 signed a formal agreement to link the United States with Mexico and Canada in a North American Union. Lou Dobbs reported this on his show on CNN in 2006 as he was horrified that our government would merge our national interests with Mexico and Canada without so much as one word of debate in the halls of Congress. This agreement has the capability to turn our three countries into something resembling the European Union. This may well be one more step to the globalization of America.

At some point in the coming years, it is likely that a world crisis (most likely economic, similar to the current one, but much worse) will lead our nation and many others to turn to the idea of a New World Order for the salvation of our countries... or at least, what our leaders believe will be their political and economic salvation. Just remember how quickly our leaders voted to spend trillions of dollars in their attempt to right the economy in the fall of 2008 and early 2009. The general public had no say in the process whatsoever. One day, something like this will happen again, but on a much larger scale, both with respect to money and numbers of nations involved. This economic problem is worldwide. Keep in mind the terrible economic plight that several members of the European Union now find themselves. One day in the future, chaotic world conditions will demand a great leader... or at least someone who appears to be one.

Rahm Emanuel, President Obama's former Chief of Staff, pointedly noted a few years ago, "The thing about a crisis --- and crisis doesn't seem to be too strong a word for the economic mess right now --- is that it creates a sense of urgency. Actions that once appeared optional suddenly seem essential. Moves that might have been made at a leisurely pace are desired instantly."[22] Hilary Clinton also suggested that a good crisis should never be wasted when she spoke at a recent gathering in Brussels, Europe.[23] Keep in mind that with the availability of the Executive Order, the President of the United States has incredible power in times of a "national emergency." It is worth taking a long look at the executive orders he has been granted during those times. The president alone has already been granted the power to change the face of America during times of emergency. Interestingly, he decides when that time exists. Therefore, it would appear that everything is in place for a one world government to come into being. All that it may take will be one more crisis to tip the scales just enough so that our country will join with others in forming this New World Order.

34. Babylon –The Great City Is Overthrown, Never To Be Inhabited Again

> **Babylon, the jewel of kingdoms,** the glory of the Babylonians' pride, **will be overthrown by God like Sodom and Gomorrah.**[20] **She will never be inhabited or lived in through all generations; no Arab will pitch his tent there,** no shepherd will rest his flocks there.[21] But desert creatures will lie there, jackals will fill her houses; there the owls will dwell, and there the wild goats will leap about.[22] Hyenas will howl in her strongholds, jackals in her luxurious palaces. (Isaiah 13:19-22)

> "Woe! Woe, O great city, **O Babylon, city of power!** In one hour your doom has come!" **"The merchants of the earth will weep and mourn over her because no one buys their cargoes any more."** Then a mighty angel picked up a boulder the size of a millstone and threw it into the sea, and said: "With such violence **the great city of Babylon will be thrown down, never to be found again."** (Rev 18:10-11, 21)

> She will be the least of the nations-- a wilderness, a dry land, a desert.[13] Because of the LORD's anger she will not be inhabited but **will be completely desolate.** All who pass Babylon will be horrified and scoff because of all her wounds. (Jer 50:12-13)

> **The Lord will have compassion on Jacob; once again he will choose Israel and will settle them in their own land.**[3]

135

> **On the day the Lord gives you relief from suffering and
> turmoil and cruel bondage,[4] you will take up this taunt
> against the king of Babylon:** How the oppressor has come
> to an end! (Isaiah 14:1,3-4)

In Zechariah 5, the prophet has a vision of a basket with a
woman in it (the woman is said to represent wickedness). The angel
told Zechariah that he was taking the basket… "To the country of
Babylonia to build a house for it. When it is ready, the basket will
be set there in its place" (Zech 5:11).

This vision came when Zechariah was speaking about what
would happen during the Tribulation. The main point is that Babylon
will have been rebuilt before or during the time of the Tribulation.
Otherwise, none of these verses would make sense. The city has to
be there in order for it to be rendered completely desolate or for the
merchants to mourn over their lack of cargoes, etc.

The preceding prophetic statements in Isaiah, Jeremiah, Zechariah,
and The Revelation, show that there will be a time when Babylon will
be overthrown by God never to rise again. In fact, this once great
city will not be inhabited in any way down through the ages after
this final destruction. Although Babylon lost the war to the Medo-
Persians, it has yet to experience the sudden obliteration of its city as
described in the above verses. As a matter of fact, the seven gardens
that were so famous still existed in some form in 25 B.C. when
Strabo, a famous geographer, visited and wrote about that city. It was
still a city of some note during the early Church Age. Even in A.D.
1100, it was significant enough to have two Mosques in it and was
even enlarged soon thereafter. Today, there are several small villages
and some newer buildings in the area that was where the ancient city
stood. Interestingly, in recent years, there has been a concerted effort
to restore Babylon to its former glory… or, close to it.

Saddam Hussein was intent on rebuilding Babylon to a level
not seen since Nebuchadnezzar. In fact, he fancied himself to be a

modern day Nebuchadnezzar. He gave it a very good start before his death in the early part of this century. The current government of Iraq wants to restore Babylon because of its rich heritage. They realize that it could become a great city and tourist attraction once again. The Future Babylon Project is now underway.

"The objective is to prepare the site and other ruins – from Ur (Abraham's birth place) in the south to Nimrud in the north – for what officials hope will someday be a flood of scientists, scholars and tourists that could contribute to Iraq's economic revival as much as oil. The Babylon Project is Iraq's biggest and most ambitious project by far, a reflection of the ancient city's fame and its resonance in Iraq's modern political and cultural heritage."[24] The United States has already contributed to its budget. The United States has refurbished a museum in Babylon and a model of the famous Ishtar Gate, the most beautiful and the most important of eight fortified gates to that ancient city. It was built during the reign of King Nebuchadnezzar. Iraq is also receiving help from the World Monuments Fund and the U.S. Embassy. Given the massive oil money available to Iraq, the continued stabilization of their nascent government and the fact that the people there want to rebuild their most famous landmark as soon as reasonably possible, it may not be long before Babylon is again an elegant, majestic city - ready to welcome tourists. That is a reasonable interpretation of the Bible verses above.

It should be noted, before leaving this topic, that there are some scholars who interpret some of these verses using the word Babylon to mean something quite different than the literal city of Babylon. They have a precedent for this as well in that during the apostolic times sometimes the word "Babylon" was a code word used to mean the city of Rome. However, a literal interpretation of the Bible does suggest that Babylon will be rebuilt in the end times... and then undergo sudden and complete destruction.

Chapter 8

END-TIMES TECHNOLOGICAL ADVANCES AND MIRACULOUS SPIRITUAL EVENTS

ARGUABLY THE TWO most important books on eschatology are Daniel and The Revelation of Jesus Christ. The prophet Daniel and the Apostle John were given incredible visions of what the end time will be like. Some of the things they saw would have been almost impossible to comprehend. Nothing like what they were being told would one day take place could possibly have occurred in their time. However, by faith, they wrote down, painstakingly, what they had seen. They figured that God would take care of the details of making His prophecy come true. After all, these visions had come straight from God and, therefore, had to be true.

The prophet Joel was given a most unusual and impressive sign by God that would allow people to know when the coming of the Lord was at hand. He was told in no uncertain terms that in the end times, God would pour out His Holy Spirit on people of all ages to let His existence and power be known. Incredibly, this has actually begun to happen all over the world... especially where Muslims dominate the landscape. Many examples of this will be given in this chapter.

Most of the prophetic signs that will be noted and discussed in the pages that follow seemingly could not have come true, without a supernatural miracle, until the twentieth century. One of them would have been practically impossible until the advent of satellite television. A universal "mark of the Beast" has been only possible for the last ten to fifteen years. The point is that it is not a pure coincidence that all of these signs of the latter days are coming together at the same time and have never done so in the past. Let us take a look at some of these technological advances and how they have become signs of the end times.

35. Worldwide Communication Will Exist in the End Times:

> **Their bodies will lie in the street of the great city**, which is figuratively called Sodom and Egypt, where also their Lord was crucified.[9] **For three and a half days men from every people, tribe, language and nation will gaze on their bodies and refuse them burial.**[10] The inhabitants of the earth will gloat over them and will celebrate by sending each other gifts, because these two prophets had tormented those who live on the earth. (Rev 11:8-10)

In the verses above, the dead bodies of two prophets during the end times will be seen throughout the world in an instant of time. That possibility did not exist until the advent of satellite television. Now, of course, it has become commonplace to broadcast important images completely around the world. Events such as the Super Bowl, World Cup Soccer, royal marriages, etc. are broadcast to every television set around the globe. During his vision of the Tribulation, John saw that the incredibly important deaths of these two prophets will be simultaneously broadcast around the world. Fifty years ago, this was not possible. Today, it is easily accomplished via satellite television or over the Internet. As with virtually all of the other signs reported in this book, the capability to see this sign become a reality has only been possible for the last few decades.

36. Preparations for the Mark of the Beast and a Cashless Financial System:

> He also forced everyone, small and great, rich and poor,
> free and slave, to receive a mark on his right hand or on
> his forehead, [17] so that no one could buy or sell unless
> he had the mark, which is the name of the beast or the
> number of his name.[18] This calls for wisdom. If anyone
> has insight, let him calculate the number of the beast, for
> it is man's number. **His number is 666.** (Rev 13:16-18)

> I saw thrones on which were seated those who had been
> given authority to judge. And **I saw the souls of those
> who had been beheaded because of their testimony for
> Jesus** and because of the word of God. **They had not
> worshiped the beast or his image and had not received
> his mark on their foreheads or their hands**. They came to
> life and reigned with Christ a thousand years.[5] (The rest
> of the dead did not come to life until the thousand years
> were ended.) This is the first resurrection. (Rev 20:4-5)

As these verses indicate, a time will be coming, during the Great Tribulation, that people will have to choose between taking the "mark of the Beast" (thereby rejecting Jesus), or staying true to Christ and, likely, dying a martyr's death. The False Prophet will command all humanity to receive this "mark" as a sign of allegiance to the Antichrist and, therefore, also to Satan. One might ask how can anyone come up with a reasonable way to place a mark on so many billions of people? Secondly, what would be the point of doing it? Let's take a look at the answer to these two questions and see why this is just one more sign of the soon coming of the Lord.

- Why would someone want to mark the body of a person? Quite obviously, if a mechanism could be found that could unmistakably identify all people "instantly" without the use of ID cards or similar items that can be copied, lost or stolen, this technique would be of significant value to a government that wants to exact complete control over its populace. By doing this, the government could control virtually anything it wanted, such as the following: buying and selling, coming and going, etc. There is no better way to do this than to place that "mark" of identity on each person's body. Obviously, this form of identification would be almost foolproof.

Everyone is aware of the fact that the world is moving toward a cashless society even now. Previously, it has been shown in another "sign of the end times," that the world is also moving toward global governance, a New World Order. When that time comes, financial transactions will typically not involve cash - if cash remains at all. Instead, simply by scanning a person, all necessary information will be obtained to enable any appropriate debit or deposit of "money" from or into their bank account. This transaction will be completed instantaneously. In some ways, this may sound great. However, there are terrible potential consequences if one despotic leader or tyrannical government controls all of these transactions.

- Once the leader of this New World Order assumes control, he will have access to modern technology to exercise that control. The ability to control the population will be greatly enhanced by the use of a micro-chip linked to a "global computer." The late anchorman, Peter Jennings, told of more than 100 Mexican law officers who had microchips implanted in their arms for the testing of this program. "Law enforcement officers in Mexico are having microchips implanted in their arms. The chips allow a person to be scanned, sort of like a cereal box at the supermarket checkout. In Mexico, this will be one more tool in the fight against crime."[25] Even the Mexican Attorney General had one implanted in his arm. These RFID (radio frequency id) chips can be scanned. A person's location can then be tracked via satellite. The VeriChip corporation recently purchased Steel Vault. They now call themselves Positive Chip. They have linked individual's health care information, via Health Link, to their credit information. This is the first time that chips have been suggested for use to track a person's economic status along with their health status.

- Until recent years, there simply was no way that any government could exact such massive control over each individual in their populace. Lately, however, this ability has been realized in the form of these miniature computer microchips. These chips have the capability to store massive quantities of information about every person. Complete financial, legal, biometric, and medical records are just some of the items that would be accessible to anyone who scans the chip. These chips are actually smaller than a grain of rice and contain more than five megabytes worth of information... plenty to contain all relevant information that any government might require to exercise control over their citizenry. Microchips have been designed to store a permanent, non-modifiable, identification number. Card scanners even now can access the implanted sensors in the chips and send information anywhere in the world instantaneously. Global positioning systems will be able to track every person. These chips have already been approved for use by the FDA and are already used in some Alzheimer patients. Every year, the capabilities of these chips become more conducive to their universal use by the coming Antichrist. They are already good enough to serve his evil purpose. It is obvious that this is the first time in world history that something like this is available... one more reason to believe that we are living in the latter days.

As the verses above from the thirteenth chapter of The Revelation note, there will come a time that the number of the Beast (666) will be inserted into the hand or forehead of every person… if that individual wants the opportunity to buy or sell things, such as food. Without this implantation, life would obviously be very difficult for all and impossible for many. For those who reject this mark, God tells them in chapter 20 of The Revelation of Jesus Christ that many will be martyred for their stand for Christ. Importantly, all those who do stand for Christ, whether they are martyred or die in some other way (while hiding out from the Antichrist) during the Tribulation, upon their death, will be ushered into heaven to live and reign with Christ. Unfortunately, those who do take the "mark" will be pledging allegiance to the Antichrist as they reject Jesus. Their eternity is sealed, and it is the same eternity as that of Satan and the Antichrist… an eternal life in hell.

37. Knowledge and Travel Will Increase at an Extraordinary Pace and Quantity:

As noted earlier, God gave his prophet Daniel, over 2,500 years ago, an amazing series of prophecies. Many of these prophecies concerned the end times… the days leading up to the Tribulation and the return of the Messiah. God also made it clear that Daniel was not going to understand all of the prophecies that he had just been given. Much of it would not become clear until the very time it was about to unfold… i.e., "the time of the end." This makes a lot of sense because many of the things that were going to take place in the last days would have seemed ridiculous to those living in his day.

> "But you, Daniel, shut up the words and seal the book **until the time of the end; many shall run to and fro**, and **knowledge shall increase**." (Dan 12:4, NKJV)

> "Go your way, Daniel, because the words are closed up
> and sealed until the time of the end." (Dan 12:9)

These verses seem to point to two main things concerning the time just prior to the Tribulation; there will be a significant increase in the speed of travel and the amount of knowledge available to mankind will be increased markedly. God would not have mentioned either of these things if they were not to undergo considerable change. It is remarkable how quickly people can travel from one place to another around the world today. From the first man, Adam, up until the beginning of the twentieth century there was not very much change in the speed of travel. Basically, the horse set the pace for all of those years. Twenty to thirty miles per hour was the speed limit that man has lived with forever... until the last hundred years or so. Now, with the advent of race cars, the airplane, and especially space travel, this "pseudo barrier" has been totally abolished... just as God foretold.

Also, in an extraordinary manner, human knowledge has exploded in recent decades. For centuries, the amount of knowledge available to man increased very slowly. At times, it actually went down... for example, in the Dark Ages. However, in the past 125 years, the quantity and quality of knowledge has increased significantly. There have been so many ways that people have tried to quantify this fact. It has been said that the sum total of human knowledge now doubles every twenty months. Maybe a better grasp on this concept can be attained if one just thinks about how much more knowledge we all have as one considers some of the following items compared to what was available in 1900:

- The inner workings of the cell (DNA, proteins, amino acids, mitochondria, etc.)
- The ability to cure many human diseases – totally new knowledge of bacteria, viruses, antibiotics, chemotherapy, etc.

- Knowledge to build airplanes, satellites, cars
- Television, stereos, computers, GPS devices
- The Internet – fast and effective spread of human knowledge – also, consider the massive amount of information that is available through the Internet. It really is amazing.
- Shockingly, even the capability to clone animals and humans is now available. This new ability of mankind has eerie similarities to the building of the Tower of Babel. In other words, many believe this activity is, in essence, "playing God."

These are just a few of the many modern developments that demonstrate the vast increase in knowledge seen in recent times. In fact, it is said that 80% of the world's total knowledge has come forth in the last ten years and that 90% of all the scientists who have ever lived are alive today. All of this is markedly consistent with the prophecies found in Daniel.

38. Jesus Will Appear to People in Dreams and Visions:

> **I will pour out my Spirit on all people. Your sons and daughters will prophesy, your old men will dream dreams, your young men will see visions.**[29] Even on my servants, both men and women, I will pour out my Spirit **in those days.** (Joel 2:28-29)

There is a very interesting phenomenon taking place in the Middle East today concerning the religious preferences of the people. As the quote from the prophet, Joel, points out above, God, through His Holy Spirit, will intervene in the lives of many individuals to demonstrate His reality and true identity in a mighty way. The Holy Spirit will be "poured out" by God in the time just before Christ returns.

As should be no surprise in the politically correct world in which we live, there are many pseudo-intellectuals among the liberal media and in the government that have concluded that Christianity is losing the battle for the minds and souls of the people of the Middle East. Wrong. Unfortunately, it is true that because of the fear of death, most people do tend to practice the Muslim religion into which they have been born. To do otherwise, requires great courage because for a Muslim to deny his faith may result in his death! Amazingly, although that is true, there still are record numbers of Muslims turning to the one true Savior, Jesus Christ, in that part of the world and every other part of the world as well. Let us take a closer look at the facts.

First of all, note some of the nonsense that is being propagated by the liberal press and media. Joel Rosenberg, the messianic Jewish scholar previously mentioned, noted in his bestseller, *Epicenter*:

- Author Charles Sennott recently wrote a book in which he made the claim that Christianity was now about to die out in the land in which it began.
- The public television network, NPR, talked of the "dwindling number of Christians in the Middle East."
- The Denver Post, in writing about the community of Christians, wrote that "in 50 years they may well be extinct."
- Sam Huntington, who wrote "The Clash of Civilizations and the Remaking of the World Order," wrote "In the long run… Mohammed wins out."[26]

The problem with all of these claims, and many more like them, is that they are simply not true. Although the religion of Islam is growing at a fast pace, Christianity is growing much faster. This topic will be reviewed later in this book in more detail. Secondly, it is absolutely true that the religion of Islam gains the vast majority of their adherents simply via birth because turning to another religion is fraught with extreme danger. Even so, amazing numbers of Muslims are still turning to Jesus as He is making it so very clear that He is "the way, and the truth and the life... [and that] no one comes to the Father, except through [Him]" (John 14:6).

Let me list just a few of the examples of Muslims turning to Christianity from Rosenberg's book, *Epicenter*:[27]

- In Egypt, 10,000 new believers worship in a "garbage village" every weekend. The *Jesus* film sold 600,000 copies in the year 2000 alone. Approximately 1.5 million copies of the Bible are sold yearly in one of many formats. These are not given away, but purchased. This means that people are very interested in learning the truth about the Lord Jesus.

- Up to 40,000 people have given their hearts to Jesus in recent years in Morocco alone.

- In Algeria, the nearly 100,000 new Christian converts have very much concerned the Islamic clerics. Laws have been passed in an attempt to terrorize those teaching about Jesus. Christians face up to five years in prison for sharing their faith. However, Christianity continues to grow in the face of this deadly opposition.

- In the Sudan, the most amazing story of people turning to Christ is seen. More than one million Sudanese have become Christians since 2000. The more they are tortured and killed by the radical Muslims, the more they turn to Christ. The Muslim clerics are horrified, but they cannot quell this growing faith in Jesus.

- In a live interview in 2001, Sheikh Ahmad Al Qataani said in an interview on Aljazeera television that six million Muslims convert to Christianity each year. Obviously, Christianity is not a religion that is dying out in the Muslim controlled nations.

- Since September 11, 2001, the known numbers of Christians in Afghanistan has grown from seventeen people to over ten thousand believers. This is in spite of severe persecution.
- Many other examples of Christian converts in Central Asia could be noted.
- Since Saddam Hussein's fall there have been at least 5,000 Iraqi people who identify themselves as Christians. Tens of thousands more are secret Christians who are understandably afraid of "coming out" openly to the general community about their new faith in Christ.
- In Iran, more people have come to Christ in the last twenty years than in the previous fourteen hundred years. In 1979, there were only five hundred known Muslim converts to Jesus. At this time, one Iranian minister told Joel Rosenberg that he believes that there are more than one million Iranians who believe in Christ as their Savior.
- "What's happening nowadays in the Muslim world has never happened before," said Father Zakaria Boutros, an Egyptian Coptic priest who is one of the foremost evangelists to the Muslim world. He says a cross-section of Muslims are accepting Jesus Christ. "Young and old, educated and not educated, males and females, even those who are fanatic."[28]

As these examples clearly demonstrate, there are very significant numbers of formerly Muslim people who are now converting to Christianity. That begs the question. Why now? Some of the credit must go to the evangelistic effort now being brought to the regions involved. This includes missionaries, television, Bibles, and films on Jesus. Also, as so many in Sudan have said, the stark contrast in the religion and God of Islam versus the religion and God of Christianity has enlightened many people to the truth of Christianity. Although all of those reasons have played a role, intriguingly, and amazingly, it seems that the main reason that many people are converting to Christianity is that Jesus is personally inviting them!

To quote Rosenberg, "What is bringing these Iranians to Christ is dreams and visions of Jesus, just as in Iraq, though in much larger numbers."[29] There are scores of examples given on many different web sites of Muslims receiving dreams and visions from Jesus that have resulted in their conversion to Christianity. It is interesting to note that when one searches the Internet for reports of *Christians seeing visions of Allah or Mohammad* there are no reports to view. On the other hand, when doing the search for *Muslims seeing visions of Christ*, there are hundreds of sites to visit. Personal testimonies of innumerable former Muslims who came to believe in Jesus as their Savior because He came to them in visions or dreams can be seen on various YouTube sites and read about on scores of other web sites. There are hundreds of examples of these incredible encounters with the living Savior. In fact, a recent Muslim survey revealed that 42% of Muslims convert to Christianity primarily due to Jesus appearing to them via dreams or visions. Other surveys reveal similar statistics. It will be worthwhile to review some of these testimonies to understand the general idea of what is causing this influx of Christianity to that region of the world:

❖ Christine Darg, author of *The Jesus Visions: Signs and Wonders in the Muslim World* states that "He is going into the Muslim world and revealing, particularly, the last 24 hours of His life - how He died on the cross, which Islam does not teach - how He was raised from the dead, which Islam also does not teach – and how He is the Son of God, risen in power."[30]

❖ Nizar Shaheen, host of Light for the Nations, a Christian program seen throughout the Muslim world, noted that, "We receive lots of letters about people who have had dreams about the Lord, visions, even miracles. When they watch the program, they say yes, we had a dream or a vision, and they accept Jesus as Lord."[31]

✧ "Probably in the last 10 years, more Muslims have come to faith in Christ than in the last 15 centuries of Islam," said Tom Doyle, Middle East-Central Asia director for e3 Partners, a Texas-based mission's agency. Many Muslim believers have said that they came to Christ after having dreams and visions of Jesus. Doyle continued, "I can't tell you how many Muslims I've met who say: 'I was content. I was a Muslim, and all of a sudden I get this dream about Jesus and He loved me and said come follow Me.' God is going into their context. But instead of finding guidance from Allah, Muslims are finding Jesus." There are so many examples of these conversions. For example, more than 200 Muslims were recently baptized during a conference in Europe led by an Iranian born evangelist, Lazarus Yeghnazar. Brenda Ajamian, a former Middle East Missionary, has also been amazed at the numbers of Muslims converting to Christianity in recent years. She said that it has "boggled her mind because missionaries have worked in the Arab world and Muslim world generally for years and without much fruit. God is at work among Muslims." Ajamian continued on to say that "churches of Muslim-background believers are growing like 'wildfire' both in the Middle East and Europe." It should be remembered that Muslims converting to Christianity in many Muslim nations can result in their imprisonment or death. That has not even slowed this great end-time move of God.[32]

✧ The dreams and visions that so many Muslim converts experience seem to fall into one of two main categories. In what many are calling a "preparatory dream," Jesus typically appears in a white robe to confirm His true identity and point out that He is the only way to heaven. The second type of encounter revolves around Jesus empowering the new convert in the face of persecution. Jesus emboldens the new believer to trust in Him for all of their needs in spite of and through any persecution that may come.[33]

✧ Another type of encounter that has been noted is neither a dream nor a vision, but often referred to as an "encounter" in these reports. For example, there was one Egyptian Muslim who was reading in the Bible where the Holy Spirit landed upon Jesus at the Jordan. As he was reading the words, "This is my Son in whom I am well pleased" (Matt 3:17), a wind broke into his room and an audible voice spoke these words, "I am Jesus Christ, whom you hate. I am the Lord whom you are looking for." The man recalls that he "wept and wept, accepting Jesus from that time."[34]

✧ Joel Rosenberg recalls another impressive encounter that a group of Iranian Muslims recently had with Jesus. When the steering wheel of the car of two Christian men who were carrying a car full of Bibles inexplicably jammed while driving down a mountain road in Iran, the driver had to slam on the brakes to avoid crashing. When the men regained their composure they heard an old man knocking on their car window. He asked them if they had the books. "What books?" was the reply. "The books Jesus sent me down here to get," answered the old man. As it turns out, recently Jesus had come to everyone in his village with the same dream to tell them to follow Him. This was followed by another dream in which Jesus told him to go down to that road at that time to pick up the "books" that would explain all about what it meant to follow Him.[35] Well, now they had their Bibles! That is quite a story... hard to believe, even. However, it is absolutely true and there are scores more examples like this that are reported in many books and on a large number of Internet sites.

❖ Since this is really not the place to continue with example after example of these incredible visions and dreams, let me suggest that those interested in learning more about this grand latter day move of God search the Internet by using the phrase, *Muslim dreams and visions of Jesus.* Then get ready to spend several hours listening, watching, and reading many fascinating testimonies of Muslim converts as they tell about their wonderful encounters with Jesus.

Summation of Prophecies Relating to Worldwide Events:

Not only did God foretell many prophetic end-time events relating specifically to His chosen people, but He also spoke of many latter day events that will affect the entire world including the Gentile nations therein. Daniel was given a vision of a one-world government that will arise out of the old Roman Empire. As the time of Christ's return nears, a worldwide economic and political system will come into existence. At some point, a very impressive, charismatic man will assume the position of world leader. This leader will be the infamous Antichrist. This world system is taking shape even now; the European Union has already become a very significant world economic force. Not only that, but there is an almost incessant call by many world leaders for a New World Order. Given the terrible condition of the current world economy, including that of the United States, it would not take much additional economic collapse for the nations of the world to turn to a world economic system as well as a New World Order of government.

Interestingly, according to the Bible, the city of Babylon will play a very important role in the latter half of the Tribulation. By that time, it will have become the economic headquarters of the New World Order. It will be a latter day Wall Street, so to speak. However, in the end times, all economic power will be centralized there – it will not be divided among various nations as it is today. Iraq has put a great deal of money and planning behind the rebuilding project of the city of Babylon. Although it still has a long way to go, great strides have been made in just the past decade. The leaders of Iraq have plans to make this once great city a beautiful tourist attraction in the near future. Of course, the Antichrist will eventually alter these plans as He will use the city for the reasons noted above.

God has provided several other signs to let the observant Christian know when His return is at hand. As mentioned earlier in this section, this is the only time in history where it has been possible for a "wake" to be broadcast around the world simultaneously. The Bible says that will happen during the Tribulation. Through satellite television and the Internet, the world will watch as the two witnesses mentioned in John's apocalyptic vision lie dead on the Temple Mount. The world will also witness their resurrection.

Almost everyone understands the prophetic significance of the coming "cashless society," and the current capability now available to give anyone and everyone a mark under their skin for identification purposes. Obviously, this relates to the "number of the Beast," 666. This plan of the False Prophet and Antichrist can be implemented even now.

The prophet Daniel foretold of a coming day when there would be a massive increase in human knowledge and the speed of travel. Sure, there was a great rebirth of knowledge, literature, and art during the Renaissance. However, only in the last hundred years, has there been an explosion of information. In every recent decade, knowledge has increased at an exponential rate. Everything, including travel and the spreading of the gospel, is also now moving at an incredibly fast pace. All of these things were foretold in the Bible to be signs of the end times.

I believe that the most amazing fulfilled end-time prophecy to be that noted by the prophet, Joel. He said that in the last days the Holy Spirit would be poured out on all flesh, old and young. The true stories of how Jesus is coming in dreams and visions to thousands of

Muslims, resulting in their conversion, is an incredible sign that His coming is very near. Even with all of these prophecies being fulfilled, Jesus, Himself, gave us many more in His Olivet Discourse. We shall review the majority of these in the next section.

Section 3:

THE OLIVET DISCOURSE: JESUS TELLS OF THE SIGNS OF HIS COMING

> As Jesus was sitting on the Mount of Olives, the disciples
> came to him privately. "Tell us," they said, "when will this
> happen, and what will be the sign of your coming and of
> the end of the age?" (Matt 24:3)

ONLY A COUPLE of days before Jesus gave His life on the cross, He was asked by the disciples to tell them what they could expect the world to be like just prior to His return. He answered them with a great sermon given on the Mount of Olives. Jesus made it clear that no one could know the specific time of His return. Even He had sacrificed that knowledge while He was living on the earth at that time. "No one knows about that day or hour, not even the angels in heaven, nor the Son, but only the Father (Matt 24:36). On the other hand, Jesus was also clear that His followers should be able to interpret the signs of the times. He had earlier reprimanded the Pharisees because they were unable to do so, "You know how to interpret the appearance of the sky, but you cannot interpret the signs of the times" (Matt 16:3).

Jesus then went on to give a fairly detailed exposition of the signs that will lead up to His Second Coming. Twelve of these signs will be presented in the following two chapters, six in chapter 9 and six in chapter 10. These end-time signs will lead up to His return to earth as the King of Kings. They can be broken up into two main topics: the spiritual, moral and religious condition of the people on the earth in the latter days (chapter 9), and the ecological and military conditions that will exist in those days (chapter 10). As will be shown, Jesus had much to say about each of these topics. Before beginning a detailed description of these signs, Jesus told His disciples to be wary of false teachers, especially those teaching in the latter days. In fact, He began this famous sermon with the words, "Watch out that no one deceives you" (Matt 24:4).

Then Jesus began His discussion on what the world could expect just prior to His Second Coming. He wanted His disciples to be ready and anticipating His return.

Note: The entire portion of the Olivet Discourse relating to the signs of the end times can be viewed in Appendix 2. Only the pertinent verses that relate to each particular sign are quoted in the chapters that follow.

Chapter 9

JESUS PREACHES ON RELIGION
IN THE LATTER DAYS

JUST DAYS BEFORE going to the cross, Jesus preached on the topic of religion in the last days. He was very concerned with what He knew was going to take place just prior to His Second Coming. For one thing, He wanted to warn everyone about the lies and deceit that would permeate much of the church. He told his disciples that there would be a significant rise in the number of false teachers in those days. Many of these charlatans will actually claim to be the promised Messiah. Others will present themselves as prophets. They all will present a false message of hope. Sadly, these people will be responsible for many people accepting a false gospel and perishing due to a lie.

Jesus also said that many of those claiming to be Christian in the end times would actually have fallen away from the true church. Many people will fall prey to the lies of Satan and charismatic world leaders armed with a seductive message that will sound convincing to many; however, this message will clearly be unbiblical. Unfortunately, many in that time will not be aware of the true message of Christ. The result will be the emergence of a worldwide apostate church. In fact, this false church will be all that is left after the true church is raptured. In fact, the apostate church will play a large role alongside of the Antichrist in the first half of the Tribulation... until he claims to be god at its midpoint and assumes absolute authority.

Although there will be a falling away from the Christian religion for many, paradoxically, this time will also be the time of the greatest revival in the history of the church. Hundreds of millions will come to know Christ as their Savior in the latter days. God will be making His last great push for converts prior to the Rapture and the Tribulation that will follow.

Unfortunately, there will also be an increase in anti-Semitism. Christians and Jews will be persecuted. Of course, as has already been noted, this hatred will result in Israel being forced into many wars. Many Christians will also pay the ultimate price for their belief in Christ. There will be a massive increase in those martyred for their faith.

Everything mentioned above is already occurring in our world today. Several examples of these things will be noted.

39. There Will Be a Marked Increase in People Claiming to Be the Messiah:

> **For many will come in my name, claiming, "I am the Christ," and will deceive many.** For there shall arise **false Christs**, and false prophets, and shall show great signs and wonders; insomuch that, if it were possible, they shall deceive the very elect. (Matt 24:5,24)

It is true that there have been people who have claimed to be the Messiah since the time when Jesus said those words on the Mount of Olives. The first known false messiah was a man named Simon Bar Cochba, a Jewish rebel commander who led a revolt of the Jews against the Romans in A.D. 132. Many Jews joined into the battle against Rome as they thought that Cochba was the actual Messiah... the kind that they had wanted and expected... a warrior. Things worked out poorly for those Jews, to say the least. The Roman Emperor, Hadrian crushed the rebellion, killing 500,000 Jewish soldiers and three million Jews throughout the rest of the Roman world. Over the following centuries, an occasional false messiah would arise, attract a following, then die. The history books suggest that about one false messiah has appeared in each century... at least those that have made enough of an impression to have made it into these books. Then came the 20th century. Things have changed dramatically.

As Jesus said in the verses above, in the end times there will be *many* who come claiming to be the Messiah (Christ). As we shall see, the number of people who have recently come on the scene with this type of claim is unprecedented. Why is that so?

The times in which we live make it very advantageous for certain charismatic individuals to convince others that they are God... or, more easily, the Messiah. There are obvious financial benefits to having people believe this lie. In some cases, the prestige and power garnered from indulging in this kind of this power trip can be very hard to resist. Up until the latter part of the twentieth century, it was very difficult to spread a messianic message to large numbers of people. Until there was television, this basically had to be done through face to face preaching. The use of books and radio may have been of some small value as well. However, this all took a lot of time, effort, and money. These are three things that most charlatans do not care to spend.

However, now that television has become a big part of our culture, many more devious men (and even women) are all too willing to delve into this medium to spread their false messianic message. A very charismatic man or woman may well be able to convince some of the ignorant and naïve people of the world that they are actually watching the true Messiah via their home television set, or within the walls of a large auditorium. Typically, the message

159

is accompanied by impressive "bells and whistles" that "hook" these lost and searching souls before they realize what has happened.

Of course, these are just a few of the logistical and practical reasons for the increased number of messianic claims in these times. It also is happening because of the spiritual environment in which we now live. Although there has been a recent surge in the number of people coming to Christ, there has also been a falling away from the Christian faith in certain areas of the civilized world. There has been a corresponding increase in false religions including the New Age belief system that has become increasingly popular in England, Europe, and the United States. There are a myriad of causes for this increase in false messiahs.

Whatever the cause in any particular case, let me mention just a dozen or so of the more infamous characters to come along in the past couple of decades. This will have only scratched the surface of charlatan messiahs:

Sun Myung Moon (Unification Church) – He came into prominence in the 1970s. Now over ninety years old, he still has a following as he claims God sent him to earth as the Messiah to complete the job Jesus started.

Charles Manson: Claiming to be the Messiah, this crazed man led followers into his web of deceit and was responsible for the cruel deaths of many (at times he claimed to be Satan as well).

Yahweh Ben Yahweh: He claimed to be the black Messiah as he told his followers that blacks were the only true Jews. God and the apostles were also black. At one time, at least 12,000 people followed him. They were, at times, willing to kill white people for him (he reportedly was responsible for killing dozens over the years). Caucasians were characterized as "white devils."

Laszlo Toth: This "Messiah" ran up to Michelangelo's "Pieta," hammered it in many places while yelling "I am Jesus Christ, risen from the dead."

Wayne Bent: God purportedly anointed him as Messiah in July, 2000. He spent most of his time as the Messiah in New Mexico while living as a polygamist. He is by all accounts a very lascivious man who has recently been convicted of criminal sexual contact with a minor.

Iesu Matayoshi: Iesu is a Japanese man who claims to be the Messiah who someday will rule over the world.

David Koresh: David is quite infamous. Recall that in 1993, his Branch Davidian religious group was caught in a standoff with the U.S. government. This eventually led to eighty of his followers dying in a fiery death in Texas. David died at that time as well.

David Icke: David is a former soccer player from England who claims to be the Messiah and lectures all around the world about the New World Order… and makes a lot of money while doing so.

Jose Miranda: Based in Miami, he claims to be both Jesus and the Antichrist. He plays both sides of the fence. He has a number "666" tattoo on his forearm.

Maitreya: He is the great spiritual teacher for our age that has been expected to arrive any time now by people such as Benjamin Crème. He is supposed to just suddenly appear at places all over the world. Crème had set up television interviews for this "Messiah" in the past, but Maitreya wasn't able to materialize for his appointed interview. Maybe next time.

Rael: A former journalist and race car driver, Rael is now a self-proclaimed Messiah. He claims to have received a message from an alien in 1973 that he was to be the Messiah for this time. After meeting with Buddha, Moses, Jesus, and

Muhammad on another planet in 1975, he wrote a book on what he learned from that meeting to share with the world.

Al Mahdi: This is a Muslim Messiah who will come at the end times. He is also known at the Twelfth Imam.

Jim Jones: In 1978, he had 909 of his followers commit suicide by drinking poisonous Kool-Aid (actually it was a similar drink named Flavor Aid). That is where we now get expressions such as, "Don't drink the Kool-Aid."

Marshal Applewhite and Bonnie Nettles: Marshal and Bonnie were the founders and leaders of an apocalyptic religious group formed in the 1970s. This Heaven's Gate New Age Cult came to an abrupt end in 1997 when thirty-nine followers committed suicide in order to leave this world on a spaceship that was hiding behind the Hale-Bopp comet. At least, that was the plan. Prior to this, many of the males, including Marshal, underwent voluntary castration. This was to help them live a more ascetic lifestyle.

There are many more people who could have been added to this list. There have been many false messiahs in recent decades… far more than at any other time in history. There are a variety of reasons for this, many noted earlier. The bottom line is that Jesus said that this increase in false messiahs will occur just prior to His return. The Rapture should not be very far away…

40. There Will Be an Explosion of False Prophets:

Many false prophets will appear and deceive many people. (Matt 24:11)

Along with the markedly increased amount of false messiahs in the world today, there are multitudes of false teachers and prophets as well. In fact, due to television, and the money available to charlatans through the use of that medium, there are more coming along every year. Note that this is just what Jesus said would happen in the end times.

Of course, there have always been a certain amount of false prophets and teachers. The Apostle Paul frequently warned the readers of his letters (in the Pauline epistles) to beware of the Judaizers. Another problem in those days was the false doctrine of Gnosticism. In both of these cases, simply put, the gospel of Jesus Christ was perverted. The gospel is not difficult to understand, nor is it only for the learned or erudite. Actually, it is quite simple and straight forward and will be addressed in some detail later. On the other hand, there are scores of religions, many even claiming to be Christian, that do not preach the true gospel of Jesus Christ. That situation has increased in recent times. Let us now take a look.

Until the mid-twentieth century, all religions tended to spread their message in essentially the same manner. There were local churches, missionaries, and, in many religions, there were evangelists. Most all religions had some form of "holy book" that they could share with interested individuals. Most often, the belief in a particular religion was passed down from one generation to the next within families. Times have really changed.

Over the last sixty years, television has changed the face of many things in the world, including religion. It has become possible in recent years to reach virtually the entire world with any given message (including religious messages) via television and the Internet. This has helped spread the true message of Christ to hundreds of millions. Unfortunately, these electronic mediums have also opened up the world to false prophets and their teachings. Some of these men and women have desecrated the truth of Jesus and His gospel for their own financial gain. Many have become truly wealthy by perverting the Word and soliciting financial donations from all kinds of people – often from those folks who could least afford it.

Some of these false prophets like to spread what has come to be known as the *"name it; claim it, gospel"* or the *"health and wealth doctrine."* This is a method used by a large number of television preachers, many of whom have become very wealthy spreading this false doctrine. This is defined by Wikipedia as "believers have a right to the blessings of health and wealth and that they can obtain these blessings through positive confessions of faith and the 'sowing of seeds' through the faithful payments of tithes and offerings."[1] Religious teachers using this technique have hoodwinked tens of millions of people. This is very unfortunate for many reasons. Many people give these miscreants much of their hard earned money – in hopes that God will bless them with even more money in return. At other times, those that have been duped give money in order that they may be healed by God. Jesus never promised His followers anything of this sort. This is just one of the sick, false doctrines that has become so popular in these latter days.

One other completely false doctrine that is perpetuated by people such as Oprah Winfrey is that there is more than one way to get to heaven. Although there is no doubt that Ms. Winfrey is a very altruistic person who has helped untold numbers of people throughout the world, she has a non-biblical view on the topic of salvation. On many occasions, the television magnate has said that there are many ways other than the Christian way to get to heaven. On her television show she said, "There couldn't possibly be just one way" to an audience member who stated that Jesus said that He was the only way. She went on to say that she was a Christian who believed "that there are many more paths to God other than Christianity." Certainly, Jesus disagreed with her. In John 14:6, Jesus said to His disciples after Thomas had specifically asked Him how to get to heaven, "I am the way, the truth, and the life. No one comes to the Father except through Me." Winfrey went on to say that Jesus came to show us "Look, I am going to live in the human body and I am going to show you how it's done."[2] She said absolutely nothing about His sacrificial death on the cross. The cross, and its incredible importance, means nothing to the typical false prophet.

Eckhart Tolle, a New Age leader and mentor of sorts to Winfrey, has the same kind of belief system. Unfortunately, there are many in the world today that are perverting the gospel in similar ways.

In addition to the New Age folks and those pushing the "health and wealth" doctrine, there are many other false prophets. These include many claiming to be Christian, such as the Mormons, Jehovah Witnesses, and Christian Science adherents. Scientology, Hinduism, Buddhism, and Islam are also religions claiming that they alone have the answer.

The question for any person comes down to which one of these multiple religious choices is the correct one? As I pointed out in the preface, only Christianity has the evidence firmly on its side. Certainly, the end-time prophecies coming to fruition in our day are further proof of the veracity of Bible. As we continue on the path toward the Rapture, these false doctrines and false teachers will only continue to grow.

41. Worldwide Apostate Church (i.e., There Will Be a Falling Away from the Church):

> Don't let anyone deceive you in any way, **for that day** (the Day of the Lord) **will not come until the rebellion occurs...** (2 Thess 2:3)

> The Spirit clearly says that **in the latter times some will abandon the faith** and follow deceiving spirits and things taught by demons. Such things come through hypocritical liars, whose consciences have been seared as with a hot iron. (1 Tim 4:1&2)

> At that time many will turn away from the faith and will betray and hate each other. (Matt 24:10)

The United States clearly was founded on Christian principals. All through the early documents of our nation, our Christian God was referenced as the foundation of the Constitution of the United States of America. People such as John Adams, George Washington, Samuel Adams, John Quincy Adams, Benjamin Franklin, Alexander Hamilton, Patrick Henry, James Madison, Abraham Lincoln and scores of others have written and given speeches extolling the necessity of building our nation on Jesus Christ and the Bible. For those who want to pursue the evidence behind this statement, just take a look at any one of many web sites that show the primacy of the Christian faith in the founding of our nation. One particularly good site is: www.eadshome.com/QuotesoftheFounders.htm

During the nineteenth century, there were great Christian evangelists and preachers in England and the United States such as Charles Spurgeon and D.L. Moody. Throughout the twentieth century, men such as Billy Sunday and Billy Graham brought the Christian message to millions of people around the world. As will be discussed later in this section, there are more people coming to a saving knowledge of Jesus Christ in recent years than at any other time in history. However, the paradox is that **there has also been a falling away from the true Christian message in those nations that had at one time been the stalwarts of the church.** Nations such as those in the European Union and the United States have fallen victim to secular humanism. This "religion" positions man as his own god... so to speak. It has been defined as *"the doctrine emphasizing a person's capacity for self-realization through reason; rejects religion and the supernatural"*[3] another definition is *"a religious worldview based on atheism, naturalism, evolution, and ethical relativism."*[4]

This apostasy began over fifty years ago, but really gained significance in the 1960s after our country legislated God out of our schools. Soon thereafter, abortion was legitimatized and legalized (1973). Homosexuality was deemed to be a totally reasonable and honorable lifestyle beginning in the early 1970s. Now, judges have taken to legislating from the bench to make homosexual marriage legal and available in more and more states. Christianity has been marginalized all throughout Europe and the United States as people, including many clergy, have embraced secular humanism as their religion. This has led to the popular religions of the day as evidenced most clearly by Oprah Winfrey. Recently, she has emerged as a leader in the New Age religion of our time. As already discussed, although claiming to be a Christian, she denies the cross of Jesus and the necessity of believing and trusting in Jesus alone for salvation.

Unfortunately, Oprah is not the only one with ideas such as this. In 1948, an organization was formed to promote unity between the religions of the world. It still exists and is known as the World Council of Churches. It is interesting that this was the same year that Israel became a nation once again. This organization is currently comprised of approximately 340 denominations, representing 500 million Christians, brought together in an attempt to unify all of these different churches. The ultimate goal is to present a statement of faith upon which all can agree. Unfortunately, therein lies the problem. Realistically, that cannot be done and still remain obedient to the Lord Jesus. His statement noted in John 14:6 would have to be ignored. There are just too many non-Christian denominations within the WCC. It is true that Jesus prayed that His disciples "be brought to complete unity to let the world know that you sent me and have loved them even as you have loved me" (John 17:23). However, Jesus did not want His followers to unite with non-Christians in a spirit of political correctness. In fact, this is made perfectly clear in the Bible...

> Do not be yoked together with unbelievers. For what do righteousness and wickedness have in common? Or what fellowship can light have with darkness?[15] What harmony is there between Christ and Belial [Satan]? What does a believer have in common with an unbeliever? (2 Cor 6:14-15)

> Avoid those "having a form of godliness but denying its power. Have nothing to do with them." (2 Tim 3:5)

> I urge you, brothers, to watch out for those who cause divisions and put obstacles in your way that are contrary to the teaching you have learned. Keep away from them. [18] For such people are not serving our Lord Christ, but their own appetites. By smooth talk and flattery they deceive the minds of naive people. (Romans 16:17-18)

David Cloud described the problem with the WCC very nicely when he wrote, "For a Bible believer, the World Council is a strange Alice in Wonderland, filled with weird nonsensical things, a place where biblical words are given different meanings. When the World Council speaks of "mission," it does not mean the mission of preaching the gospel of Jesus Christ to the unsaved; it means, rather, striving for world peace, economic justice, and such. Further, the World Council can present different faces, depending on the situation. In some places it tries to appear more "evangelical" in theological outlook when the majority of local pastors are of that persuasion, but in other instances its true liberal face is unveiled. There is probably no heresy that has not been broached within the context of the WCC. We could describe the error of the WCC under a wide number of categories. We could speak of its theological Modernism, its Marxism, its secular Humanism, its Feminism, its Sacramentalism, its Syncretism [the fusion of two or more different belief systems into one], and its Universalism. The simple fact is that the WCC fails every biblical test that could be applied. It is patently and grossly unscriptural."[5]

Dozens of examples of this heretical syncretism could be cited. However, let the following five suffice:

1. In 1993, the WCC sponsored a group of approximately two thousand radical women in a conference in Minnesota

blatantly "seeking to change Christianity." Speakers included those such as Chung Hyun Kyung, a Korean who equates the Holy Spirit with ancient Asian deities and Virginia Mollenkott, an avowed pro-abortion lesbian. Amazing heresies came forth in that conference. For example, Mollenkott said at one point that she "can no longer worship in a theological context that depicts God as an abusive parent [referring to Christ's death on the cross] and Jesus as the obedient trusting child." During a panel discussion on Jesus, Delores Williams of Union Theological Seminary, said: "I don't think we need a theory of atonement at all. I think Jesus came for life and to show us something about life. I don't think we need folks hanging on crosses and blood dripping and weird stuff... we just need to listen to the God within."

2. At the seventh assembly of the WCC, this organization once again bowed to political correctness as they opened the meeting by allowing Australian aboriginals to perform their traditional purification ceremony while dancing around an altar in their nature worship rite. The leadership of the WCC played along with this absurd heathen demonstration. "WCC General Secretary Emilio Castro asked permission for the council to enter the land. Gathered in the tent were Aboriginal elders, who ritually granted permission, whereupon the WCC worship leaders walked in procession into the tent."

3. The WCC published a book in 1984, No Longer Strangers. In this book, names for addressing God in worship were suggested. These included Lady of Peace, Lady of Wisdom, Lady of Love, Lady of Birth, Lord of Stars, Lord of Planets, Mother, Home, and Bakerwoman. God is not a woman.

4. Most egregious are the repeated statements to the effect that Jesus is not the only way to the Father. There are many examples of this heresy that could be mentioned. They all

are similar to the statement issued by Wesley Ariarajah, a Methodist preacher, who said in 1987, "It is necessary to leave the idea that all other religions are living in darkness... can a Christian turn around and say to the Buddhist that he or she is misguided to think this about the Lord Buddha? We have no grounds to do so." A few years later, he added, "My understanding of God's love is too broad for me to believe that only this narrow segment called the Christian Church will be saved."

5. In a meeting in 2003, the moderator, Aram I said that Christ "goes beyond Christianity. We must understand other religions are part of God's plan for salvation and are not a mission field." Dr. Ralph Colas, executive secretary of the American Council of Christian Churches, concluded his report on that meeting with "The change of leadership in the WCC only furthers the continuation of fulfilling their goal of building a visible one-world church. The WCC seeks to weld together apostate Catholics and Protestants with compromising Evangelicals and Pentecostals."[6]

It is apparent that this very large organization, the WCC, is accepting of essentially any kind of religious theology. It does not espouse a Christine doctrine. In fact, their all-inclusive program is more aligned with secular humanism. Of course, there are still many true Christians within the WCC. However, realize that after the Rapture of the church, all people that are left behind will be non-Christian, initially. It will be at that time that this large and all-inclusive world religious organization will likely provide the structure for the apostate church that is prophesied in the Bible to gain a powerful position during the first portion of the seven year Tribulation.

So we see that over the course of the last sixty years, secular humanism has gained marked prominence as a ruling belief system in the United States, Canada, and European nations. Much of the world that used to be at the forefront of Christianity has succumbed to this apostasy through its association with the heresies put forth by the World Council of Churches.

This is the situation that Jesus and Paul told us would exist just before the return of the Lord. Paradoxically, as will soon be shown, it is also true that millions are coming to Christ in these last days. An intriguing situation, but one also prophesied two thousand years ago.

42. There Will Be an Increase in Those Martyred for Their Faith in Jesus:

> "Then you will be handed over to be persecuted and put to death." (Matt 24:9)

In the two thousand years of the Church Age, approximately seventy million faithful Christians lost their lives because of their faith in Jesus. Sixty-five percent of these martyrs died within the last one hundred years.[7] This is quite an intriguing fact. While there are so many in the world today who like to think that we are working our way to an idyllic New World Order, nothing could be further from the truth.

Anti-Christian forces in places such as Indonesia, Bangladesh, Nazi Germany, Turkey, India, Nigeria, East Timor, Cuba, many of the former Soviet Republics, Saudi Arabia and several other Muslim countries have murdered countless saints during the past century. The virtual genocidal martyrdom in Rwanda and Burundi in the 1990s produced more martyrs than at any other time period in history. An average of 160,000 Christians have been martyred yearly since 1990 according to Antonio Socci, an Italian journalist who has studied this subject extensively.[8] In today's world, places such as Nigeria, Algeria, the Sudan, and Pakistan are major contributors to this number.

Socci also noted that Communism and Muslim Fundamentalism are the greatest fuels for this persecution of Christians in the modern world. Lately, this has been most severe in the Sudan.

Although it is difficult to believe for those Christians who live in relative religious peace in the United States, it is true that millions of their brothers and sisters around the world suffer greatly, even unto torture and death. As the Bible prophecies, as the end times approach, there will be a great turning against the church in the world with increasing persecution of Christ's followers. Although this persecution is already horrendous, it will become even worse after the Rapture for anyone who chooses to follow Jesus Christ. However, God forbid if any other decision is made by those who are left behind for their eternal destiny is at stake.

43. Rise of Anti-Semitism:

You will be hated by all nations because of me. (Matt 24:9)

Jesus was speaking to His Jewish disciples when He made this statement about the end times. Today, Israel and the Jewish people face unparalleled hatred from other nations and peoples of the world.

It is important to keep in mind that Israel and its people were really not looked at very much differently by the other nations of the world before the time of Christ. Sure, they were involved in wars with other nations such as Assyria and Babylon. Later, they had to struggle against the Greeks and Romans. However, there was no particular hatred from any country against the people of Israel simply because of their origin (with the exception of the people who were the descendants of Ishmael and Esau, for example, the Edomites who were the descendants of Esau). After the time of Jesus, however, anti-Semitism began to rise. The Romans expelled the Jews from their land in A.D. 70, as they trampled the city of Jerusalem and completely destroyed the Temple. In A.D. 135, Hadrian continued the persecution when he murdered hundreds of thousands of Jews and even renamed their homeland, Palestine.

Later, with the proclaiming of Christianity as the state religion of Rome, some early Christian fathers came out against the Jewish people. St. Augustine wrote that they were a "wicked sect" and should be banished because of their evil.[9] Others called them Christ killers because of the role of some Jews in the crucifixion of Christ. In Norwich, England in 1140 A.D., a superstitious priest and an insane monk charged a local Jewish man with killing a Christian child in order to procure Christian blood for the preparation of matzo bread for a Jewish holiday. This false and absurd charge begat even further attacks against the Jewish people. The Crusaders and the Muslims also trained their sights on the chosen people of God. Jews were even blamed for instigating the Black Death by poisoning wells even though they were dying just like all the others. Even Martin Luther was an anti-Semite as he wrote a treatise entitled, "Of Jews and Their Lies" in which he said that their synagogues should be set on fire. All through the ages since the death of Jesus, Jews have been a target for the rage of many people.

Incredibly, a book published in the late nineteenth century, *The Victory of Judaism over Germanism* by Wilhelm Marr, postulated that Jews were genetically different than Germans and therefore could never be assimilated into the German race. In 1879, he founded the League of Anti-Semites. This was the first German organization committed to expelling the Jews from Germany. During the late nineteenth century in Austria, many Jews rose to the top of several preferred professions, such as law and medicine, making themselves a further target for jealousy and rage. Hitler was a youth at this time, and he also learned to hate the Jews. This, of course, led to the zenith of anti-Semitism when so many people went along with Hitler as he carried out the Holocaust of six million Jews. He could not have done it without so many people and countries looking the other way, seemingly giving their tacit approval through a lack of opposition.

Anti-Semitism still runs rampant in the world today. A recent survey in Spain revealed that one in three Spaniards is anti-Semitic.[10] Thirty to forty percent of Germans in another recent survey were also found to harbor anti-Semitic feelings. That is particularly disappointing considering what happened in WWII.[11] Sweden reported a 57% increase in anti-Semitic crimes last year in their country with 250 crimes against Jews being committed (i.e., simply because the person was a Jew).[12] Scotland reported that this type of crime increased by 300%. In Canada, anti-Semitic incidents reached record levels in recent years. The important point is that all over the world anti-Semitism is prevalent, and is *gaining more ground every year,* apparently without much opposition.

Just think about the reaction in the world community to the situation between Israel and the Palestinians. The reaction is really incredible. Every nation other than the United States (and sometimes England, Canada and Australia) is either silent concerning the conflict between Israel and the Palestinians, or they take the side of Palestinians. Israel is constantly being castigated by the United Nations. In my review of over 225 resolutions by the United Nations that relate to the current situation between the Palestinians and Israel, I found no resolution that condemned any action by the Palestinians – not for any of their suicide bombings, their incessant attacks from Gaza with bombs landing on Israel almost daily (even though Israel gave up Gaza so this would not happen), and so many other breaches of previously agreed-upon ceasefires. On the other hand, Israel was "condemned" by scores of resolutions by the United Nations. "The tiny nation of Israel has much less than one-half of one percent of the world's population, yet she takes up about a third of the UN's time and energies, mostly resulting in condemnations. The UN still passes about thirty anti-Israel resolutions every year. The UN, who should be the paragon of fairness, has often openly supported Israel's enemies. When Israel pushed into Lebanon in 1982 to root out the PLO, it was amazed to find the UN facility there was being used as a terrorist training base. Such a thing has happened on more than one occasion. It was UN vehicles that were recently used in the Hezbollah kidnapping of three Israeli soldiers on the Lebanon border."[13] The whole situation is remarkably absurd. There does not seem to be any reasonable, logical explanation for the consensus of world opinion against Israel. Therefore, I suggest that this "upside down" viewpoint must be satanically inspired.

One fact that seems to be ignored by all of the nations of the world is the attitude of the Palestinians with respect to Israel. For example, the Justice Minister, Freih Abu Medein, came out with the following edict on May 5, 1997, "The death penalty will be imposed on anyone who is convicted of selling one inch of land to Israel. Even middle men involved in these deals will face the same penalty." On May 16, Palestinian Authority leader Yasser Arafat said, "We are keeping track of land dealers and punishing them."[14] In fact, many Arab realtors have been killed for doing just that. These murders did not elicit any significant outcry or condemnation from the United Nations or any other individual nation. It seems that it does not matter how the Jews are treated. Nothing at all, including terrible hate speech, suicide bombings, daily missile attacks from Gaza, or anything else seems to be enough to bring the world community to the defense of Israel and the Jews even though they inhabit just a fraction of their biblically promised land.

The simple fact is that the Jews are hated by many people in the world today. God said that Jews would be hated and, indeed, they are. They are His chosen people, but God has obviously allowed them time to see how they will fare without His guidance and help. The answer is quite obvious. God will bring even more judgment upon them during the Great Tribulation – in order to bring them back to Him. God will bring record numbers of Jews back into His "fold" during that time. They will finally recognize Jesus as the Messiah, and God will lead them into the promised Millennial Kingdom at the conclusion of the Battle of Armageddon.

One more point should be made clear. God has always said that those that bless Israel will be, in turn, blessed. However, it is also true that those who curse Israel… will be cursed. All nations, including the United States and those who live therein, should heed these words.

44. Kingdom Preached to the Entire World:

And this gospel of the kingdom will be preached in the whole world as a testimony to all nations, and then the end will come. (Matt 24:14)

"Turn to me and be saved, all you ends of the earth. (Isaiah 45:22)

Jesus told His audience on the Mount of Olives just a couple of days before His crucifixion that, just before His return to earth, the gospel will have been preached throughout the entire world "as a testimony to all nations." Of course, the "good news" of Jesus' wonderful sacrificial death was only known locally in the decades following His death. Even after the spread of Christianity throughout the majority of the Roman Empire, most of the remainder of the world remained totally unaware of the person and work of the Son of God. Before this gospel message was spread any further, civilization entered into the Dark Ages. Almost a thousand years passed before the Renaissance once again gave hope to the world. With the invention of the printing press, the Bible's "good news" was made available to many more people, and the ember of hope grew and spread.

Over these last several hundred years, dedicated missionaries and Bible translators have worked to spread the gospel to every continent. However, it has only been since the invention of satellite television and the Internet that the gospel of Jesus Christ has truly been preached "in the whole world." Every nation has now been reached by the gospel message concerning our Lord. Let us take a look at some recent data that proves this point.

Grant Jeffrey pointed out in his book, *Armageddon: Appointment With Destiny*, that almost fifty percent of Africans have become born again Christians within the last century. Given that only three percent were Christian at the onset of the twentieth century, it is amazing how things have changed in our time. Indonesia is another excellent example of the growth of Christianity in recent years. Although mostly Muslim, twenty percent have recently accepted Christ as Savior. Russia now has over one hundred million Christians living within its borders. Koreans had rejected Christ almost without exception as World War II began. Now, fifty percent are believers. As has been pointed out in an earlier *sign*, Muslims have turned to Christ in surprisingly vast numbers over the past couple of decades.

China may be the greatest example of this end-time conversion to faith in Christ. In 1950, after over one hundred years of continuous missionary intervention, there were only one million Christians in all of China. Quite a price was paid by many for trusting in Jesus. For over one hundred years there have been tens of thousands of Christian martyrs in China. For example, in the infamous Boxer Rebellion, at the turn of the twentieth century, 239 foreign missionaries and more than 32,000 faithful Chinese believers were butchered simply because they were Christians.[15] However, even though the penalty for following Christ in that communist country is still very severe (tens of thousands of Christians have been martyred under their communist rule), approximately 125,000,000 have turned their lives over to Jesus in recent decades. Most of this has had to take place in the underground church. These people intensely crave the Word of our Lord and are willing to risk their very lives to hear the gospel and to learn how to live for the Lord.

Jeffrey also noted that the Lausanne Statistics Task Force on Evangelism revealed even more impressive details on the growth and spread of the gospel in recent years:

- In 1430, one percent of the world was Christian
- In 1790, two percent called themselves Christians
- In 1940, three percent of people were Christian
- In 1997, ten percent were Christian – and this percentage has risen even faster over the last decade

In other words, it took 510 years to increase from one to three percent, but only 57 years to go from three to ten percent. In total numbers, this may be even more impressive. In 1934 there were 40 million evangelical Christians. Today there are approximately 650 million.[16]

Religious broadcasters now reach every language group throughout the world. Wycliffe translators have translated the Bible into 3,850 languages reaching over 98% of the world's population. The gospel of John has been translated into virtually every human dialect in the world.[17]

The World Christian Encyclopedia estimates that there are 125,000 new Christians each day. In this past decade, there has been a net gain of approximately 42,000,000 Christians every year. With the ever increasing rate of evangelization, estimates are that one billion more people will become Christians in the next decade. Evangelical Christianity is growing at the fastest rate of all.

Although Islam is increasing rapidly in the world today, studies show that Christianity is increasing at almost twice its rate. Why? For one thing, there are more than eighty thousand missionaries currently spreading the gospel throughout the world. More importantly, the message concerning the Christian God is true. For another, as Muslims emigrate away from their home countries and become "westernized," they are finally able to hear the logical arguments behind the Christian message. Without the fear of being disowned or even beheaded, they are able to make a reasoned decision. However, as discussed earlier, the most amazing reason behind many of these conversions to Christianity is that Jesus is appearing to significant numbers of Muslim people in dreams and visions. The Lord tells them that He is the only way to salvation. Because of this, millions of Muslims have recently accepted the gospel message. Jesus said that the end would come when His gospel message was preached throughout the world. That time is at hand.

Chapter 10

ECOLOGICAL DISASTERS AND DEVASTATING WARS IN THE END TIMES

J ESUS WAS VERY cognizant of the downward spiral the world would experience as His Second Coming approached. With the increase of false religion, there will be a corresponding increase in immorality. Biblical absolutes will no longer be honored as truth. The world will descend toward the inevitable judgment of God.

Jesus said that there will be many signs that will allow students of the Bible to recognize the coming Tribulation. Famine and disease will become more devastating than at any other time in history. Millions will die, even before the Great Tribulation. Earthquakes, a sign of judgment often used by God, will increase in number, size, and effect. Many people and cities will endure the terrible devastation that often accompanies major earthquakes.

As noted in the previous chapter, a sharp dichotomy will exist between increasing numbers in the true church and those embracing the developing, ungodly, apostate religion. Jesus warned us to expect a terrible increase in immorality. The lack of godly wisdom throughout much of the world in the latter days will result in many devastating wars. Jesus seemed to strongly suggest that nuclear war will be a reality in these days. In fact, He said that if not for His return, the world would not survive the end-time wars. Given our knowledge of the power of nuclear warfare, it is clear that the world could not survive an all-out nuclear exchange. Unfortunately, with so many insane "suicide" terrorists living on the earth today, it is difficult to see how nuclear war can be avoided indefinitely. However, Jesus does give His followers a very real hope. He truly will be the salvation of this world as He leads His followers into the world to come.

45. Wars and Rumors of Wars:

> **You will hear of wars and rumors of wars**, but see to it that you are not alarmed. Such things must happen, but the end is still to come.[7] **Nation will rise against nation, and kingdom against kingdom.** (Matt 24:6,7)

The twentieth century showed a dramatic increase in the number and scope of wars in the world. Of course, there have been two world wars. The Red Cross estimates that over 100 million people have died in armed conflict since 1901.[18] Other estimates go as high as 200 million.[19] In 1993 alone, there were twenty-nine major wars fought.

War has been, unfortunately, a common event all through the ages. However, since WW II there has been a war somewhere on this earth at all times... usually more than one. Sixty million people died in WWII alone.

The most terrible aspect of modern warfare is the very real possibility of total annihilation of great numbers of people - even, the entire planet if enough nuclear bombs explode. Biological and chemical weapons of mass destruction have also made a big impact on the world, beginning primarily in WWI. They have made a big comeback in recent years and pose a major threat to the world today.

The nations of the world have armed forces with hundreds of millions of soldiers, ready to go to war at any time. Grant Jeffrey noted that almost fifty percent of the world's scientists are working on weapon-related research. Forty percent of all scientific funding goes to arms research. China is expanding its army at an incredible rate. China is also selling more tanks and other armaments to Africa than all western countries combined as it can produce these arms at a fast pace and cheaper than the western countries.[20] Not only is Africa joining in this arms race, but the Arab countries are buying great quantities of weapon systems as well. Iraq has purchased a significant amount of fire power from Russia in recent years, including much nuclear material and information. Muslim Arab nations are now a threat to stability in Europe. Very soon, Iran will have the nuclear bomb. The United States has sold large quantities of arms to Israel as well as many Arab nations. Israel has developed many of her own weapons as well. Many are weapons of mass destruction.

WMDs are in the possession of numerous countries, some of whom are very likely to use them without much thought of the ultimate consequences. Jeffrey stated that there was "one military weapon and the equivalent of four thousand pounds of explosives for every man, woman, and child worldwide."[21] Keep in mind that there are over six billion people. Even if he is off in his calculation by a factor of ten, this is still an amazing quantity of destructive power. Much of it is in the possession of people who are certainly less than emotionally stable… and that is using very kind terminology.

To give an idea of the power of modern weapons, one Trident missile can launch from 10,000 miles away and detonate within 100 yards of the target. The explosive power carried on just one submarine is greater than all of the fire power delivered during WWII by both sides combined.[22] Over 1.5 trillion dollars is spent on armaments each year worldwide, $698 billion by the United States in 2010 alone. Approximately, $70 billion worth of weapons are sold between nations every year as well.[23]

The relatively newly developed Electro Magnetic Pulse (EMP) Weapons can paralyze a nation such as the United States for up to three months. Computers, businesses, television, cell phones, most other communications, railways, airports, and any other power generated system would shut down immediately. Experts say that it would take months or even years to return the power to normal in the United States. The United States economy would be devastated and its military would take a serious blow. Terrorist groups could get the capability to launch this form of weapon from North Korea, China, Russia or Iran (soon to have it) either directly or by theft. The weapon could be delivered by a Scud missile from a ship in the shipping lanes off the coast of the United States. Scud missiles have become a common weapon among terrorist nations and organizations. They are available on the weapons market at a modest price.

The biggest concern about future wars on earth relates to the massive increase in devastating power of the weapons currently available for use by so many nations and individuals. This fact is one of the major reasons I believe that the coming of Jesus will be in the near future. **There has never been the development of a weapon system that has not eventually been used in some manner and by someone.** The United States used the Atomic Bomb in WWII. Chemical weapons have been used many times now (e.g., in WWI, and by Iraq against the Kurds and Iran). Someone or some people used biological weapons against the United States (anthrax) immediately after 9/11/2001. There are other examples that could be cited as well. The point is that **someone, probably a rogue terrorist, will someday use a nuclear bomb against some nation.** Likely, they will use more than one. **This may well trigger a massive nuclear response.**

As with virtually all of the other signs noted in this book, this dire situation, predicted to arise just before the coming of the Lord, has only been existent in recent times. In fact, prior to WW II the possibility of total global destruction was not feasible. It has only been within the last twenty years that there came into the world lunatics with the capacity and the desire for worldwide destruction and the annihilation of significant segments (i.e., billions of Jews and Christians) of the populace.

Without the intervention of the Messiah when that destruction begins, or very soon thereafter, the world would come to an end. However, the Bible does tell us that Jesus will intervene and put a stop to all of the death and destruction... and lead us into the Millennial Kingdom of peace.

46. Famines:

> **There will be famines and earthquakes in various places...** (Matt 24:7)

There have been people who have gone hungry in every generation of the historical record. However, there is no denying that the current world hunger situation throughout the world is unprecedented. Just taking a look at recent United Nations reports shows the massive problem of famine in many nations. In just the last year, the United Nations has stated that **one billion people suffer from hunger.** This is an increase of over 100 million hungry people over the last five years, primarily due to the financial crisis in which the world now finds itself. Two billion people are considered at risk. **Fifteen million people die of starvation every year.**[24] **Six million are children.**[25]

Food aid is at a twenty year low. The director general of the Food and Agricultural Organization (FAO), Jacques Diouf, said that the level of hunger "poses a serious risk to world peace and security."[26] Almost 20% of the world goes to bed hungry every night. If one adds those in the sub-Saharan Africa with those in the Asia-Pacific region, almost one billion people are undernourished. Kostas Stamoulis, the director of the FAO, noted that "it is the first time in human history that we have so many hungry people in the world."[27] The head of the World Food Programme (WFP), Josette Sheeran, said the world may be reaching a point where the global system can no longer cope with the massive numbers of malnourished people.

Places such as Darfur, Ethiopia and Somalia are in critical need of food resources. However, nowhere near enough is being produced. An estimated 3.7 million people, which is over 50% of the population, in Somalia are malnourished. Recent drought conditions have made this rebel-controlled nation even more desperate for food.[28] One in six children is considered acutely malnourished (requiring specialist care). These children are in danger for their lives every day, according to the FAO.

There is no reason to expect that these things will get any better. Deserts are increasing at a rate of fifteen million acres per year. Tens of billions of tons of topsoil are being lost annually as well. Forests are being cut down at an alarming rate. Coupled with the population growth (over 225,000 people added per day), the diminished food supply is a disaster that shows all signs of only growing much worse.

A closer look at the rate of population growth is in order. From Adam until Jesus, the population grew from one to 300,000 people. From Jesus until the beginning of WWI it grew to 2 billion people. In 1962, the population reached 3 billion; 5 billion in 1980; 6 billion in 2000; 7 billion today. It has grown exponentially.[29] The world's growth rate peaked in the 1960s at 2% with a doubling time of thirty-five years. Currently, the doubling time has been reduced to sixty-one years. However, even at that lower rate, the world population would reach 13 billion by 2067.[30] Providing enough food for a population that is even close to that number of people is very difficult to imagine. Take a look at the graph that follows:

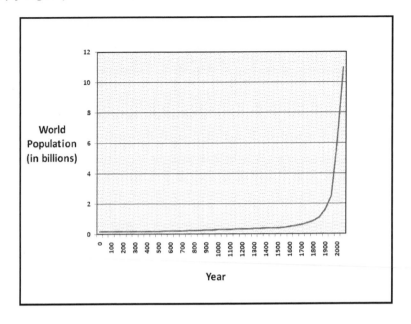

World Population (in billions)

Year

Figure 11: World Population from time of Christ to present

One of the many things that Jesus stated concerning the time just before His return was the fact that so many people would be suffering from famine. Famine is unfortunately a very serious and rapidly increasing problem in our world today.

47. Pestilence:

And there will be great earthquakes in various places, and famines and pestilences. (Luke 21:11)

The increase in famine in the world has just been discussed, and the amazing increase in the number and severity of earthquakes will be soon noted. Jesus also told his audience just before His crucifixion that the world would see a very serious problem of *pestilence* during the time of the Tribulation. Webster's dictionary defines pestilence as "a contagious or infectious epidemic disease that is virulent and devastating." There have always been serious infectious diseases in the world. However, the world has reason to be very concerned that a particularly devastating, lethal, and very contagious disease may be just around the corner. Let us take a look at this problem in the world today.

Probably the best example of how quickly an infectious disease can appear and yield devastation and death is seen in the viral agent commonly referred to as AIDS. This terrible disease made its appearance in the very late 1970s and began its inexorable scourge on the populace immediately. It took three to four years to identify the culpable viral agent and decades to reach a point where there is some hope for those who get infected... if they are treated early enough and without cessation. An estimated 24 million people died as a result of contracting the AIDS virus between 1980 and 2007. Over 2 million died worldwide just last year. An estimated 22.4 million adults and children in sub-Saharan Africa are currently infected with HIV. 14.1 million children have lost one or both parents to the AIDS virus and 1.8 million children have the virus themselves. Worldwide, 35 million people are believed to be infected with this virus. There are still 2.6 million new infections each year.[31] There is still no cure for AIDS even though it has been over thirty years since it claimed its first victim. 75 million people are projected to die from the AIDS virus by 2030.[32] This is just one example of a new infectious disease in our world. There are many others. There are also many old diseases that are currently causing massive damage as well.

Dysentery kills millions of people around the world. It is a terrible disease. Avian influenza (H5N1) continues to cause deaths worldwide. Over one-half of the cases have proven fatal.[33]

Malaria kills approximately one million people yearly.[34] It is one of the worst infectious diseases on the planet today. Tuberculosis has made a comeback and potentially could become a serious killer again. The problem is that a drug resistant strain has recently developed. Only time will tell how this will spread among the populace.

Many other infectious diseases are mounting a terrible comeback at this time. For many years it looked as if drug therapy would wipe out these killers. Unfortunately, these bacteria and viruses have the capability of mutating and becoming even more potent killers, and many have already done so. One of many examples is MRSA, Methicillin Resistant Staph Aureus. This has become the scourge of hospitals around the nation in recent decades as it is often hospital acquired and very, very difficult to eradicate. It can be deadly.

One other important point is that many infectious agents are now switching over from their typical animal (non-human) host and becoming infectious to humans (such as the AIDS virus). In a *Newsweek* magazine interview, Mary Pearl, president of the Wildlife Trust, explained: "Since the mid-1970s, more than 30 new diseases have emerged, including AIDS, Ebola, Lyme disease and SARS. Most of these are believed to have moved from wildlife to human populations."[35] Others include bird flu, swine flu and the West Nile disease. That is what is so worrisome about the H5N1 influenza. All it would take would be for a deadly infectious agent, such as HIV or H5N1... or any such agent, viral or bacterial... to come onto the world scene, as so many already have recently, plus be as easy to spread as the common cold. Imagine the devastation that would result. These types of infections have begun to appear in recent decades. All it will take is the "perfect storm" of an easily transmittable, lethal infectious agent to devastate multiple hundreds of millions in very short order... and there really would be little, if anything, we could do about it.

Although the AIDS virus has been the most destructive plague the world has ever seen, there are currently many other infectious agents that cause great concern. The biggest recent worry was noted in a recent article in *National Geographic* (Oct. 2005), where it was reported that deaths from a widespread bird flu pandemic could range from "7.4 million to an apocalyptic 180 million to 360 million."[36] A really big problem today is the ever increasing global travel that allows for infectious agents to travel from one continent to another in a matter of hours. If any one of the many influenza viruses ever again becomes extremely virulent, mass death will quickly result. Consider that in 2009, one in six Americans became infected with the Swine flu. What if that had been extremely deadly?

In addition to the infectious agents noted above, in recent decades there has been an ever increasing problem coming from the introduction of chemicals into the earth and atmosphere. Although the statistics may well be influenced by political bias, it is definitely not a good thing when the Toxic Substance Strategy Committee reported to the President of the United States in 1980 "that the cancer death rate in the United States had increased sharply and … occupational exposure to carcinogens is believed to be a factor in more than 20 percent of all cases of cancer."[37] Not only that, but the inappropriate discarding of these carcinogens is believed to contribute greatly to the significant increase seen in cancer cases and deaths in the general population.

Jesus tells us in His Olivet Discourse that in the days leading up to His return, the world will experience an increase in these devastating diseases. With the arrival of the Great Tribulation, this increase in pestilence in our world will become a significant component of God's judgment upon the earth.

48. Earthquakes:

> There will be famines and **earthquakes** in various places.
> All these are the beginning of birth pains. (Matt 24:7-8)

It is quite incredible to look at the statistics concerning the increase in large earthquakes during recent years. The chart below will show the marked increase seen over the last ten years of earthquakes with a magnitude of 7.0 or greater on the Richter Scale. It is important to point out that this magnitude earthquake has been tracked for over a century so that there is no doubt that the world has seen a huge increase in recent years.

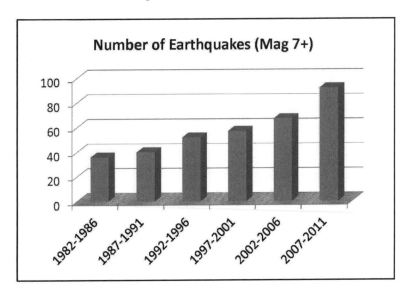

Figure 12: Number of Earthquakes from 1982 to 2011

In the last five years, there have been ninety-two magnitude 7+ earthquakes, showing that the pace continues to increase (e.g., there have been forty-five in the last two years alone which was far more in two years than any five year period in the 1980s). When considering the more powerful and destructive category 8+ earthquakes, the increase in recent years is even more obvious. There were six of these terrible events in the 90s, but fourteen in the first decade of this century. That is an increase of over 133%. There have been three "Great" (over 9.0 on the Richter scale) earthquakes in the past eleven years. These are terribly devastating natural disasters. Geologist Robert McCaffrey recently determined that, under typical circumstances, there should be only one to three category 9 or greater earthquakes per century... certainly not three per decade.[38] It is quite obvious that something very strange is happening. Six of the ten largest earthquakes on record have occurred since Israel became a nation again in1948. Three of these were in the past seven years. Note also that the graph above demonstrates that these devastating earthquakes have increased by almost 300% from the early 1980s to the last five year average.

As has also become quite obvious in this last decade, terribly destructive tsunamis often accompany these huge earthquakes. Two of the most destructive tsunamis in history have occurred in the past seven years (Indonesia in 2004, Japan in 2011).

Before leaving this topic on natural disasters, it is intriguing to note that the world has experienced in the past two years an inordinate number and severity of tornados. Although tornados were not specifically mentioned as a sign of the end times by Jesus, He did say that along with earthquakes, famine and pestilence, there would also be "fearful events and great signs from heaven" (Luke 21:11). "There were 1,897 tornadoes reported in the US in 2011 (of which at least 1,706 were confirmed). 2011 was an exceptionally destructive and deadly year for tornadoes; worldwide, at least 574 people perished due to tornadoes … The 550 confirmed fatalities is also the second-most tornadic deaths in a single year for tornadoes in US history."[39] "Several tornado records were broken in 2011, including for greatest number of tornadoes in a single month (758 in April) and the greatest daily total (200, on April 27). On Sunday, May 22, 2011, an EF-5 tornado [also referred to as an *incredible* tornado] hit the city of Joplin, Mo., leaving an estimated 157 people dead. The Joplin tornado is the deadliest single tornado since modern recordkeeping began in 1950. The EF-5 tornado had winds in excess of 200 MPH, and was ¾ of a mile wide, and had a track lasting six miles."[40] Dr. Jack Hayes, the director of the National Weather Service said, "In my four decades of tracking weather, I have never seen extreme weather like we had in 2011. In the past, we've had years of extreme flooding, hurricanes, or snow storms, but I can't remember a year with record-breaking extremes of nearly every type of weather."[41]

Unfortunately, 2012 has begun with another flourish of destructive tornadoes. As of March 5, "the U.S. as a whole already stands at 163 tornadoes above the 2005–2011 national average for the current date, which is only 124."[42]

In summary, this recent significant upsurge in all of these severe weather events, especially the marked increase in the number of major earthquakes, is what one would expect to observe just prior to the Second Coming of Jesus.

49. The Love of Most People Will Grow Cold:

> **Because of the increase of wickedness, the love of most will grow cold.** (Matt 24:12)

> But mark this: There will be terrible times in **the last days.**[2] People will be lovers of themselves, lovers of money, boastful, proud, abusive, disobedient to their parents, ungrateful, **unholy,**[3] **without love**, unforgiving, slanderous, without self-control, **brutal,** not lovers of the good,[4] treacherous, rash, conceited, **lovers of pleasure rather than lovers of God**--[5] having a form of godliness but denying its power. (2 Tim 3:1-5)

This prophecy made by Jesus is a very difficult one to quantify. In fact, it is almost impossible to do so. On the other hand, if one just thinks about these statements by Jesus and Paul and then takes a moment to reflect on the times in which we live, I believe that it will not be hard to recognize that wickedness is increasing around our nation and world. As these verses state, this has been the result of the fact that the warm, natural love that many people should be expected to have for one another (especially their own spouse and children) has "grown cold."

Let us take a look at just a few things as representative examples:

a) **Abortions:** This is one of the more egregious sins taking place in the world today, and suggests strongly that we are living in the last days. It is difficult to believe that our Lord will allow this horrific murder to continue unabated. And, it looks like the only way for it to stop is for Jesus to stop it Himself.

Just take a look at the number of abortions that take place every year. An incredible forty-two million lives in this world are snuffed out every year; approximately 115,000 each day. Due to unsafe medical conditions around the globe, abortions result in seventy thousand maternal deaths and five million disabilities per year.[43] It is estimated that between one-half and one-third of all pregnancies end up with an aborted baby. Sadly, nearly one-third of American women will have an abortion at some point in their lifetime. Over two-thirds of the women involved identify themselves as Christian.[44] This cannot be something that God will tolerate much longer. It is ridiculous that our Congress cannot pass a law to make even horrific partial-birth abortions illegal. In these cases, babies that are obviously viable are ripped apart while their head remains inside their mother's womb. If they were allowed to come out of the womb first, then this killing would be called what it is - first degree murder. However, because of our absurd laws, if the infant is killed while its head is still inside the mother, it is not technically murder. Unbelievable! How can so many people be so icy cold in our world today? Approximately, 95% of all abortions are performed because the birth of that particular baby is stated to be "inconvenient" by the mother. Only one percent of abortions are due to the woman having been raped.[45] It should go without saying that this is an issue that is new to this current generation. Prior to the early 1970s, there were only relatively few abortions performed. However, today that number has exploded. This, again, is what one would expect to find as Christ prepares to return for His people.

b) **Murder:** Even murder is now done at a rate and for reasons that show the deterioration of our society. For example, there are thousands of prisoners being murdered every year in China (and other countries such as India) just to harvest their organs for use in other people. This is a thriving business. For example, a kidney may bring fees ranging from $3 thousand to $20 thousand. As discussed in another area in this section, millions of people are murdered each year for all sorts of absurd and hateful reasons – such as what is euphemistically called "ethnic cleansing." Another recent addition to the list of murders committed is the "suicide bomber." Muslim extremists have convinced many thousands of their countrymen and women that it is a wonderful idea to bomb themselves and others to expedite and assure their own trip to heaven (where the men will be met by seventy-two willing and beautiful virgins) while helping Islam dominate the world for Allah. One final point... virtually every day one can read about some heinous murder that happens in most every reasonably sized city in America. No longer do most of these murders shock people... because today these murders are all too commonplace.

c) **Homosexuality:** Of course, homosexuality has always been an issue, including in biblical times. What we see happening in our world today is *the acceptance of this deviant sexual practice as normal*. This was not the case until the early 1970s. Before that time, homosexuality was always considered as pathological and treated as such. Although I have no problem with those who say that people are born with homosexual tendencies (this may well be true in some, or even many, cases), I differ with their conclusion. The Bible says that engaging in homosexual acts is a sin. There is nothing in the Bible to suggest that it is justifiable to engage in homosexual acts as long as the person was born with those tendencies. Just as it is a sin to engage in fornication (including sex before marriage or adultery), even if there is a natural urge or tendency to do so, it is also a sin to *practice* homosexuality. There may also be a natural tendency to lie and cheat for many if not all people – yet, lying and cheating are sins. Therefore, the fact that a person may be born to desire a person of the same sex, is not an excuse to act on this desire. This would still be a sin. God says we are not to sin.

d) **Sexual immorality:** It is quite apparent to everyone over the age of sixty that sexual immorality in the United States rocketed upward beginning in the 1960s. This is also true in Europe and Great Britain and much of the remainder of the world. All one has to do is look at the modern day barometers of movies and television to see how accepted the breaking of God's sexual laws has become. In fact, in our world today, sexual immorality is accepted as normal behavior. As such, it is typically not looked upon as a sin. However, God sees it as a sin, just as He sees homosexuality as a sin.

e) **Angry, brutal people:** Although reports vary, most studies say that between one and two million children are abused each year in the United States alone. Sixteen percent of women have undergone the horrible experience of rape or attempted rape in the United States at some point during their lives.[46] Hundreds of thousands of children are abused each year across the world. Most of these cases go unreported.

White slave trading is another horrific example of the depths to which so many have sunk in our increasingly immoral world. Places such as Thailand, Japan, Israel, Belgium, Germany, Turkey and the United States are common destinations for these human "slaves." The major source countries for these women slaves are Thailand, China, Nigeria, Bulgaria, Belarus, Moldova and Ukraine. Estimates are that over 800,000 people are sold into this horribly degrading form of slavery every year. This problem has increased exponentially in the past decade. It has become a major funding source for organized crime.[47]

f) **Childhood Pornography and Prostitution:** The use of children in the heinous acts of prostitution and pornography by evil adults is incredible and hard to believe. For example, in India, approximately 1.2 million children are forced into prostitution. Hideously, these children are sold for sex more than ten times per day! About 40% of all prostitutes in that nation are children.[48] That is the same percentage estimate given by the authorities in Thailand. In so many parts of the world, child prostitution is tolerated by the authorities. The thought is that if a child is over the age of twelve, and if the child does not file a complaint, no crime has been committed. There has been the development of a child sex industry in recent decades. Sex tourists pay to travel to certain countries in order to engage in all sorts of sordid sex acts with children. Of course, this type of activity is amazingly evil and destructive and filled with all manner of mental and physical consequences for these victimized children who are robbed of both their innocence and childhood. Thailand, Cambodia, India, Brazil, and Mexico are the leading countries providing this horrific immoral activity to perverts around the world.

In summary, the main point here is that over the last forty to fifty years, the morality of people in the United States and in most of the world has eroded significantly. The immoral activities in our world have escalated to levels that are shocking to anyone who has even reasonable moral standards. However, many people today have become hardened to sin and immoral activities. They have become "lovers of pleasure, rather than lovers of God." That is why very little is being done to rectify most of these terrible abuses. This is what we would expect if we are living in the latter days. In fact, Jesus did say that this would be the case just prior to His return. Jesus will be coming to correct this deplorable situation very soon.

50. Doomsday Weapons and the Melting of the Elements:

> Blow the trumpet in Zion; sound the alarm on My holy hill! Let all who live in the land tremble; For the day of the LORD is coming, it is close at hand -² A day of darkness and gloom, A day of clouds and blackness, Like dawn spreading across the mountains... **Before them fire devours, behind them a flame blazes. Before them the land is like the Garden of Eden, behind them a desert waste; nothing escapes them.** (Joel 2:1-3)

> For then there will be great distress, unequaled from the beginning of the world until now – and never to be equaled again. ²² **If those days had not been cut short, no one would survive.** (Matt 24:21-22)

> But the **day of the Lord will come as a thief in the night.** The heavens will disappear with a roar; **the elements will be destroyed by fire, and the earth and everything in it will be laid bare...** ¹² That day will bring about the destruction of the heavens by fire, and **the elements will melt in the heat.** (2 Peter 3:10,12)

The description given here by Peter is a pretty good way of describing the melting of the elements due to the effects of a nuclear holocaust. Indeed, the earth will be on fire and everything in the path of the massive blast will melt with incredible heat. Things

197

will dissolve. Matter will melt. The prophet Joel gives us another glimpse of the destruction left behind after a nuclear blast.

The energy produced by a nuclear explosion is millions of times more powerful than conventional explosives. The temperatures reached are in the tens of millions of degrees. When there is a surrounding material such as air, rock, or water, the radiation rapidly heats it to an equilibrium temperature (i.e., the same temperature as within the bomb). This causes vaporization of surrounding material resulting in its rapid expansion and a massive shockwave. The effects are devastating and difficult to imagine. Indeed, the elements actually "will melt in the heat!" This is what the Bible tells us will happen just before Jesus Christ comes again.

In fact, Jesus told us in His Olivet Discourse that unless He came and shortened the time of this terrible Great Tribulation, all of humanity would be destroyed. Thankfully, He will come and usher into the Kingdom all those who have placed their trust in Him.

Summation of End-Time Signs Described in Olivet Discourse:

In his address on Mount Olivet, Jesus spoke on the topic of His Second Coming. He told His listeners that the world will deteriorate into very perilous times as that day approached. Jesus warned that many alive in those days will experience terrible famine and pestilence. The world will begin to experience an ever increasing number and severity of earthquakes. Instead of the realization of a New Age of peace and harmony that some still believe mankind will one day bring onto this earth, the world has been plagued by continual war. Never has our world seen the number and severity of wars as has been experienced in recent history.

There will be an unusual contrast concerning religion in the end times. Although the gospel will finally be spread throughout the entire world, there will also be a marked increase in apostasy. The number of faithful Christians will increase to unprecedented numbers. However, false messiahs and false prophets will spread

Satan's lies to all those who will listen. Much of the world will abandon its moral compass... with devastating results. Christians will be hated and martyred throughout the world. In fact, millions will die because of their love of Jesus. Anti-Semitism will also be a hallmark of this age. Simply put, the battle between good and evil will reach its zenith.

Since all of these signs are seen in the world today, it is surely reasonable to believe that the Second Coming of Jesus is close at hand. Let us not forget that Jesus gave us all of these signs so we would be prepared for His coming. In fact, He said that when all of these things began to occur, to "stand up and lift up your heads, because your redemption is drawing near" (Luke 21:28).

CONCLUSION

THERE ARE SO many things happening in the world today that strongly suggest Jesus will soon return. The Bible gives its reader many different signs so that people can know when that time is close at hand. Although Jesus is clear about the fact that no one will know the day or hour of His return, He also says that people can and should be aware of the *season* of His return. This book was written to reveal fifty of the signs that demonstrate the world is currently in the end times. It is highly likely that many in the generation alive today will witness the Second Coming of the Lord.

Why would God give mankind all of these end-time signs? He obviously wants people to be aware of and prepare for the things to come. Remember that the world as we know it will one day suddenly change forever when the Lord comes to rapture His saints into heaven. That wonderful event will be followed by a seven year period of Tribulation, the likes of which the world has never seen. At the conclusion of this terrible period of time, Jesus Christ will return to this earth, defeat the forces of evil, and set up a glorious Millennial Kingdom. Finally, God will introduce a new heaven and new earth where those who have committed their lives to Jesus will spend eternity in perfect peace and joy with Him forever. Admittedly, that sounds incredibly fantastic. Yet, it is absolutely true.

The Bible says that it will happen, and the Bible is the actual Word of God. I implore any remaining skeptic to research the books listed in Appendix 3 carefully. Millions of people have come to a strong belief in the Bible after a careful evaluation of the facts. God says that He will honor those who seek Him. **"You will seek Me and find Me, when you search for Me with all your heart"** (Jer 29:13). I personally have many friends who have become Christians after living as atheists far into their adult lives. There is no doubt in my mind that the major reason for unbelief in the Bible is the stifling combination of human pride coupled with laziness. Many people have too much pride to question their unbelief and/or are too lazy to prayerfully read the Bible along with the many excellent books that demonstrate the veracity of the Bible. This is an eternally fatal mistake.

Although it is certainly of interest and value to contemplate the future of the universe, it is infinitely more important and profitable to consider the future of the individual. *What will happen to you when you pass from this life into the next?* As a doctor for almost forty years, I have had the opportunity to ask hundreds of patients this question. I am not the bashful sort. Unfortunately, the answer is almost always the same. At least 80% of the answers go something like, "I hope I am going to heaven. I have lived a good life." Sadly, this is even the answer that many professed Christians give. This is definitely not the pathway to heaven revealed by the God of the Holy Bible. Since so many apparently do not know the path from this life to an eternity in heaven, let me now take the time to answer this extremely important question. What did the Lord Jesus Christ have to say on this matter?

Almost two thousand years ago, there was a very intelligent Pharisee, named Nicodemus, who understood that Jesus came from God with an important message to share to the world. He went to Jesus one night to inquire about these important questions concerning life and eternity. Jesus told him, "I tell you the truth, no one can see the kingdom of God unless he is born again" (John 3:3). Nicodemus did not understand the meaning of this remark, so Jesus continued on to explain that each person must have a *spiritual rebirth* in order to gain entrance into heaven. Jesus continued on to further explain with this most famous statement, "For God so loved the world that He gave His only begotten Son, that whoever believeth in Him shall not perish but have eternal life" (John 3:16). The ultimate importance of this belief was then revealed when Jesus continued with, "Whoever believes in Him is not condemned, but whoever does not believe stands condemned already because he has not believed in the name of God's one and only Son" (John 3:18). His disciple, Thomas, asked for further explanation on the pathway to heaven on the eve of the Lord's crucifixion. Jesus replied, "I am the way and the truth and the life. No one comes to the Father except through me" (John 14:6).

Just a moment later Philip asked Jesus to show the disciples God, the Father. Jesus replied, "Don't you know me, Philip, even after I have been among you such a long time? Anyone who has seen me has seen the Father … Don't you believe that I am in the Father, and that the Father is in me? … Believe me when I say that I am in the Father and the Father is in me; or at least believe on the evidence of the miracles themselves" (John 14:9-11). Here, and in many other verses, we see Jesus explaining that He is God incarnate. Interestingly, Jesus also points to the fact that He has performed many miracles to prove that He is actually God the Son. The very next day, Jesus allowed Himself to be sacrificed on the cross for the sins of mankind. Just before He passed on from this life to the next He said, "It is finished" (John 19:30). Jesus was referencing that He had just accomplished His major task, that of reconciling a sinful mankind to a Holy God. All that remains is for the individual to recognize that he/she is a sinner, repent, and accept God's free gift of salvation.

Jesus came to earth and accomplished several important tasks:

- He came and gave us a model of how to live our lives while on this earth,
- He came and proved through His words and actions that He was God incarnate.
- Most importantly, Jesus came and lived a sinless life, thus enabling Him to be the required perfect, unblemished, sacrifice for the sins of mankind.

Remember, Jesus said that in order to gain eternal life in heaven, a person must believe in Him. Believing in Jesus, is not just recognizing that He was a person of history. Satan does that. Instead, it is accepting by the historical evidence and by faith that Jesus was exactly who He claimed to be (i.e., God) and accomplished what He came to do. Jesus is an equal member of the Holy Trinity who sacrificed His life on the cross for all those who will place their trust in Him for their salvation.

On Easter morning, Jesus was resurrected from the dead. He had prophesied that he would defeat death and Satan in exactly this manner on several occasions during His life on earth. It was no coincidence that He became the "first fruits" of salvation on the Jewish Festival of First Fruits. On that same Easter Day, the Jews celebrated their first spring harvest by waving a sheaf of their first harvested barley toward the God of heaven. Of course, much more barley would immediately follow in the harvest. In the same manner, Jesus was the first of a large harvest that was to follow Him into heaven. Saints such as Abraham, David, Moses, Job, and many, many more were sure to quickly follow Jesus. Everyone who places their faith in Jesus will also follow Him into heaven one day.

Approximately seven weeks after that Easter morning, the Christian Church began on the next Jewish festival, Pentecost – again, this was not a coincidence. Jesus sent the third person of the

Holy Trinity, the Holy Spirit, to abide within all those who place their faith in Jesus. The Holy Spirit was called the "Counselor" or "Helper" by Jesus. "If you love me, you will obey what I command. [16] And I will ask the Father, and He will give you another Counselor to be with you forever—the Spirit of truth. The world cannot accept Him, because it neither sees Him nor knows Him. But you know Him, for he lives with you and will be in you" (John 14:15-17). This wonderful gift of the Spirit of God immediately gave tremendous power to the Apostles. All these men had such incredible faith after witnessing the resurrection of their Savior, Jesus, that they spent the remainder of their lives evangelizing their world. In fact, the evidence suggests that all (with the exception of John) eventually died a martyr's death after a life of faithful service to the Lord of heaven. One should take a moment to inquire why all of these men, and many other witnesses of the crucifixion, would die a martyr's death if they had not also witnessed the resurrected Jesus. Maybe there would be one, or even two, lunatics that would die for a blatant lie, but certainly not dozens of men and women. That idea makes no logical sense at all. Yet, all of these men spent the remainder of their lives telling people that they had walked and talked with the risen Lord. These men obviously had seen and spoken with the resurrected Son of God.

Three thousand people became Christians on the day of Pentecost - an auspicious beginning for the church. This troubled the Jewish hierarchy greatly. Along with the Romans, the Pharisees thought they had heard the last of Jesus. Both quickly found that was not going to be the case. Therefore, the leaders of the Jews placed a young, brilliant Pharisee in charge of shutting down this new religious sect. He was known as Saul of Tarsus. Saul was highly effective in his new position. Showing initiative, as he would throughout his lifetime, he eventually travelled north to Damascus in order to put down a burgeoning Christian community in that city. Along the way, Saul had an incredible encounter with Jesus.

Although the Bible goes into much interesting detail in describing this meeting and the days that followed, the result was that Saul became an ardent believer that Jesus was the promised Messiah, God the Son. In fact, in the thirty years subsequent to that conversion, Saul (later God changed his name to Paul) became arguably the greatest Christian evangelist and teacher that ever lived. God eventually chose Paul to write a large portion of the New Testament, while under the inspiration of the Holy Spirit. "All Scripture is God-breathed, and is useful for teaching, rebuking, correcting, and training in righteousness" (2 Tim 3:16-17). He wrote many epistles (letters) to several of the churches of that time. Through these letters, Paul taught these new Christians many things relating to living the Christian life. His major emphasis, however, was to make sure that every believer was completely cognizant of the full meaning of the gospel of Jesus Christ. As is the case today, there were false teachers in the early church who were trying to pervert the gospel. Therefore, Paul carefully explained the gospel message through his teaching and letters. This critically important New Testament teaching points the way to reconciliation between sinful man and Holy God. It teaches us how to be saved, to live forever with God and His saints in heaven. A summary of the gospel message follows:

- "**Man is destined to die once, and after that to face judgment.**" (Heb 9:27)
  The Bible clearly maintains that every person has but one life to live. Upon death, everyone will one day stand before God and answer for their actions during their life on earth.
- "**For we will all stand before God's judgment seat.** [11] It is written: "'As surely as I live,' says the Lord, '**every knee will bow before me; every tongue will confess to God.'**" [12] So then, **each of us will give an account of himself to God.**" (Romans 14:10-12)

Sooner or later everyone will bow before the Lord Jesus Christ. One day, everyone will recognize that Jesus is the Messiah, God the Son. It will be a terrible thing to do this for the first time when meeting Him at the judgment – that will be too late.

- "for **all have sinned and fall short of the glory of God**, [24] and are **justified freely by His grace through the redemption that came by Christ Jesus.** [25] **God presented Him as a sacrifice of atonement through faith in His blood.** He did this to demonstrate His justice..." (Romans 3:23-25)

  "For the wages of sin is death, but the gift of God is eternal life in Christ Jesus our Lord." (Romans 6:23)

  No one other than Jesus can live a life of sinless perfection. Yet, no one who has committed a sin may enter heaven... at least until the penalty for their sin has been paid. God has provided a solution through the Lord Jesus Christ, His only Son.

- **"God made Him who had no sin to be sin for us, so that in Him we might become the righteousness of God."** (2 Cor 5:21)

  In God's justice system, after living a sinless life on earth, God (in the person of Jesus Christ) is able to substitute Himself and pay the penalty for the sins of a repentant sinner. If we turn to Jesus as our Savior, God credits us with His righteousness. In a sense, when God looks at a Christian, He sees the perfect righteousness of Jesus.

  "Though your sins are like scarlet, they shall be as white as snow." (Isaiah 1:18)

- "But God demonstrates His own love for us in this: **while we were still sinners, Christ died for us.** [9] Since **we have now been justified by His blood**, how much more shall we be saved from God's wrath through Him." (Romans 5:8)

  As already noted above, the penalty for sin is death. Jesus paid the penalty for the sins of mankind when He died and shed His blood on the cross. All those who turn to Him in faith are forgiven their sins. They will be saved from an eternity in Hell. This is the most wonderful free gift of God. **No one can earn it.** However, a **person must accept this gift by faith.** How is this done? Paul explained this in his letter to the Romans...

- **"That if you confess with your mouth 'Jesus is Lord,' and believe in your heart that God raised Him from the dead, you will be saved.** [10] For it is with your heart that you believe and are justified, and it is with your mouth that you confess and are saved... [13] For *'everyone who calls on the name of the Lord will be saved.'"* (Romans 10:9-10,13)

  "Therefore, there is now no condemnation to those who are in Christ Jesus." (Romans 8:1)

  All God asks from anyone is that they turn to Him in faith, ask for forgiveness for their sins, believing what the Bible says about the life, death, and resurrection of Jesus. Remember, God gave the world many proofs for the truthfulness of His Scriptures. The evidence for the resurrection of Jesus is tremendous. God wants and requires that we turn to Jesus in faith and believe. He certainly did not mean this to be a leap of faith... only a small step of faith. That is why God gave us so much evidence to believe in this gospel message and His Son.

- **"And if the Spirit of Him who raised Jesus from the dead is living in you, He who raised Christ from the dead will also give life to your mortal bodies through His Spirit who lives in you."** (Romans 8:11)

  "And if anyone does not have the Spirit of Christ, he does not belong to Christ." (Romans 8:9)

  "Having believed, you were **marked in Him with a seal, the promised Holy Spirit, who is a deposit guaranteeing our**

inheritance until the redemption of those who are God's possession – to the praise of his glory." (Eph 1:13-14)

God explains that once we accept Jesus as our Lord and Savior, His Holy Spirit abides within us while we pursue sanctification throughout the remainder of our lives on earth. The indwelling Spirit of God is our guarantee of the eternal inheritance that God has promised to everyone who believes. It should be the goal of all believers to allow the Holy Spirit control over every aspect of their lives. The more successful a Christian is in this endeavor, the more peace and joy they will experience in this life on earth. In any case, all believers are promised a truly wonderful eternal life in heaven.

- "Therefore, since we have been justified through faith, **we have peace with God through our Lord Jesus Christ."** (Romans 5:1)

  After receiving Christ as Savior and Lord of our life, a person can rest assured that their eternal destiny is secure. This destiny is incredible, indeed. Take a look at just a few of God's promises for the future of the believer...

  "... we are God's children. Now if we are children, we are heirs – heirs of God and co-heirs with Christ..." (Romans 8:16-17)

  "I am convinced that neither death nor life, neither angels nor demons, neither the present nor the future, nor any powers, [39] neither height nor depth, nor anything else in all creation, will be able to separate us from the love of God that is in Christ Jesus our Lord." (Romans 8:38-39)

  "He [God] will wipe every tear from their eyes. There will be no more death or mourning or crying or pain, for the old order of things has passed away." [5] He who was seated on the throne said, "I am making everything new!" (Rev 21:4-5)

These are only a few of the wonderful promises God has for those who follow Him.

The Bible claims that Jesus is God Incarnate and that He came to earth primarily to be sacrificed for the sins of the world – to reconcile lost sinners to Himself. Jesus said that in order to secure forgiveness of sins and gain eternal life in heaven, a person must turn to Him in faith and be "born again." Paul explained this gospel message in further detail.

Philosophers often ponder questions such as the *"What is the meaning of life?"* and *"What is truth?"* I suggest that Jesus is Truth and the meaning in life can be found when we make Jesus the center of our lives… when He is made the Lord and Savior of our life.

The decision a person makes concerning the Lord Jesus is, of course, monumentally important. This decision will change your eternal destiny. God gave us all the free choice to either choose Him or reject Him. When we pass from this life into the next, we will all meet Jesus. He will either welcome us into our heavenly reward, or He we will stand before Him in judgment.

Please consider all of the evidence carefully and prayerfully. Read His Word, the Bible, and understand His message of love and salvation. Remember that all Scripture is inspired by God. Do not continue to postpone this decision, as no one is promised tomorrow. In the last book of the Bible, The Revelation of Jesus Christ, Jesus said, "Here I am! I stand at the door and knock. If anyone hears My voice and opens the door, I will come in to him and eat with him, and he with Me" (Rev 3:20). Jesus loves you and died so that you might be saved. Today is the day of salvation.

APPENDIX 1:
DANIEL'S PROPHECY OF THE
SEVENTY WEEKS

S INCE THIS BOOK discusses the many signs currently
being seen in the world today that lead up to the seven year
Tribulation, a brief discussion of where this period of God's judgment
is introduced in the Bible may be in order. The last book of the New
Testament, The Revelation of Jesus Christ, goes into great detail
explaining the events that will take place during this time... and
thereafter. In addition, God initially revealed many aspects of His
future plans for Israel and the world to the Old Testament prophet
Daniel. In fact, the overall framework of this seven year Tribulation
was given to Daniel while he was in earnest prayer.

As Daniel's life was drawing to a close, he prayed to God
to have mercy on His chosen people. Daniel was saddened and
perplexed that even after almost seventy years of captivity, his
people still remained enslaved in Babylon. He was aware of the
prophet Jeremiah's prophecy, "This country will become a desolate
wasteland, and these nations will serve the king of Babylon for
seventy years" (Jer 25:11). He also knew of another prophecy of
Jeremiah, "When seventy years are completed for Babylon, I will
come to you and fulfill my gracious promise to bring you back to this
place [Jerusalem]" (Jer 29:10). Very soon after this prayer by Daniel,

King Cyrus issued the decree that allowed for the Jews to return to their beloved city, Jerusalem… just as God had prophesied over 150 earlier, "[God] says of Cyrus, he is my shepherd and will accomplish all that I please; he will say of Jerusalem, 'Let it be rebuilt,' and of the Temple, 'Let its foundations be laid'" (Isaiah 44:28).

While Daniel was still in prayer, God dispatched the angel Gabriel to provide that faithful, elderly prophet with a sweeping prophecy concerning Israel. Daniel had shown great concern about God's plan for Israel (Daniel's people) and God was about to lay out His future plans for the Jews. Although God was going to honor His promise and allow them to return and rebuild their Temple in very short order, He was about to reveal a grand prophecy concerning the future of Israel and its relationship with the Messiah. God did this through Gabriel in a vision often referred to as the *Seventy Weeks of Daniel*. It is important to know that a "week" of years is equivalent to seven years. The King James Bible opens Daniel 9:24 with the words, "Seventy weeks." This important prophecy (Daniel 9:24-27) gives detailed information concerning the future dealings of God with His chosen people.

> "Seventy 'sevens' [70x7=490 years] are decreed for your people and your holy city to finish transgression, to put an end to sin, to atone for wickedness, to bring in everlasting righteousness, to seal up vision and prophecy and to anoint the most holy." (Dan 9:24)

God told Daniel exactly what He would accomplish during the 490 year period beginning with the decree to rebuild Jerusalem. At the conclusion of this period of time, God will have accomplished everything noted above; He will then anoint the Messiah as King of Kings and Lord of Lords, and the Millennial Kingdom will begin. A decree to rebuild Jerusalem was given to Nehemiah in 445 B.C. In these verses, the actual time that Christ would come into Jerusalem for His final appearance and crucifixion is given.

This time is measured "from the issuing of the decree to restore and rebuild Jerusalem until the Anointed One [Jesus], the ruler, comes, there will be seven 'sevens,' and sixty-two 'sevens'" (Dan 9:25). In fact, this historic event occurred at the conclusion of the first sixty-nine periods of seven years (i.e., 483 *prophetic years* – 360 days per year) as measured from the time Nehemiah was given the decree to rebuild Jerusalem. Sir Robert Anderson is often credited with working out the math to show that this prophecy did, indeed, come true.

"After the sixty-two 'sevens,' the Anointed One will be cut off and will have nothing [Jesus will be rejected by the Jews and crucified]. The people of the ruler who will come will destroy the city and the sanctuary [The Romans destroyed the Temple and Jerusalem in A.D. 70]. The end will come like a flood: War will continue until the end, and desolations have been decreed. He will confirm a covenant with many for 'seven.' In the middle of the 'seven' he will put an end to sacrifice and offering. And on a wing of the temple, he will set up an abomination that causes desolation, until the end that is decreed is poured out on him" (Dan 9:26-27). The last few verses reference the Antichrist, who will broker a peace treaty with Israel and their enemies at the onset of the Tribulation, desecrate the Temple 3 ½ years later, and then be defeated by Jesus Christ at the conclusion of that seven year period.

Some may wonder why the last seven years of the 490 year period outlined in Daniel 9 does not begin until after the Rapture... after the church is removed from the earth. The reasoning goes as follows:

After the death and resurrection of Jesus came the current time in which we live, the Church Age. During this period, God is dealing primarily with the church, not the nation of Israel. For this reason, there is a "break" in the counting of the seventy "sevens." This break came after the first sixty-nine weeks concluded with the rejection and crucifixion of Jesus. Certainly all Jewish people are welcomed into the church, but most Jews have yet to recognize that Jesus is the Messiah. The final seven year period is known as the Tribulation and will come after the Church Age concludes. This period (from year 483 to year 490) will begin at the onset of the Tribulation, right after the Rapture of the church. At that time God resumes dealing primarily with the Jews.

The Tribulation period will immediately precede the onset of the Millennial Kingdom and will be the time that God uses to judge unrepentant mankind and bring His chosen people back into harmony with Him; Israel will finally understand that Jesus is the actual Messiah. Also, the Bible tells us that God will send His Son, Jesus, at the conclusion of this Great Tribulation to defeat the Antichrist at the Battle of Armageddon and then usher in His Kingdom. Many other books of the Bible, such as The Revelation, Zechariah, Ezekiel, and Isaiah, go into great detail concerning what will happen during the Tribulation and the Millennium. Jesus adds much additional information in His Olivet Discourse.

APPENDIX 2:
SELECTED PORTIONS OF JESUS'
OLIVET DISCOURSE

J ESUS' OWN WORDS in His Sermon on the Mount of Olives just before He went to the cross give the most complete information concerning the state of the world just before He comes back to the earth to rescue the world from Satan and his demons.

Signs Leading Up to His Second Coming

Watch out that no one deceives you. ⁵ For many will come in my name, claiming, 'I am the Christ, 'and will deceive many. ⁶ You will hear of wars and rumors of wars, but see to it that you are not alarmed. Such things must happen, but the end is still to come. ⁷ Nation will rise against nation, and kingdom against kingdom. There will be famines and earthquakes in various places. ⁸ All these are the beginning of birth pains. ⁹ "Then you will be handed over to be persecuted and put to death, and you will be hated by all nations because of me. ¹⁰ At that time many will turn away from the faith and will betray and hate each other, ¹¹ and many false prophets will appear and deceive many people. ¹² Because of the increase of wickedness, the love of most will grow cold,¹³ but he who stands firm to the end will be saved.

¹⁴ And this gospel of the kingdom will be preached in the whole world as a testimony to all nations, and then the end will come. ¹⁵ "So when you see standing in the holy place 'the abomination that causes desolation,' spoken of through the prophet Daniel—let the reader understand—¹⁶ then let those who are in Judea flee to the mountains. ¹⁷ Let no one on the roof of his house go down to take anything out of the house. ¹⁸ Let no one in the field go back to get his cloak. ¹⁹ How dreadful it will be in those days for pregnant women and nursing mothers! ²⁰ Pray that your flight will not take place in winter or on the Sabbath. ²¹ For then there will be great distress, unequaled from the beginning of the world until now—and never to be equaled again. ²² If those days had not been cut short, no one would survive, but for the sake of the elect those days will be shortened. ²³ At that time if anyone says to you, 'Look, here is the Christ!' or, 'There he is!' do not believe it. ²⁴ For false Christs and false prophets will appear and perform great signs and miracles to deceive even the elect—if that were possible. ²⁵ See, I have told you ahead of time. ²⁶ "So if anyone tells you, 'There he is, out in the desert,' do not go out; or, 'Here he is, in the inner rooms,' do not believe it. ²⁷ For as lightning that comes from the east is visible even in the west, so will be the coming of the Son of Man. ²⁸ Wherever there is a carcass, there the vultures will gather. ²⁹ "Immediately after the distress of those days "'the sun will be darkened, and the moon will not give its light; the stars will fall from the sky, and the heavenly bodies will be shaken.' ³⁰ "At that time the sign of the Son of Man will appear in the sky, and all the nations of the earth will mourn. They will see the Son of Man coming on the clouds of the sky, with power and great glory. ³¹ And he will send his angels with a loud trumpet call, and they will gather his elect from the four winds, from one end of the heavens to the other. ³² "Now learn this lesson from the fig tree: As

soon as its twigs get tender and its leaves come out, you know that summer is near. [33] Even so, when you see all these things, you know that it is near, right at the door. [34] I tell you the truth, this generation will certainly not pass away until all these things have happened. [35] Heaven and earth will pass away, but my words will never pass away.

The Coming of the Messiah

[36] "No one knows about that day or hour, not even the angels in heaven, nor the Son, but only the Father. [37] As it was in the days of Noah, so it will be at the coming of the Son of Man. [38] For in the days before the flood, people were eating and drinking, marrying and giving in marriage, up to the day Noah entered the ark; [39] and they knew nothing about what would happen until the flood came and took them all away. That is how it will be at the coming of the Son of Man. [40] Two men will be in the field; one will be taken and the other left. [41] Two women will be grinding with a hand mill; one will be taken and the other left. [42] "Therefore keep watch, because you do not know on what day your Lord will come. [43] But understand this: If the owner of the house had known at what time of night the thief was coming, he would have kept watch and would not have let his house be broken into. [44] So you also must be ready, because the Son of Man will come at an hour when you do not expect him. [45] "Who then is the faithful and wise servant, whom the master has put in charge of the servants in his household to give them their food at the proper time? [46] It will be good for that servant whose master finds him doing so when he returns. [47] I tell you the truth, he will put him in charge of all his possessions. [48] But suppose that servant is wicked and says to himself, 'My master is staying away a long time,' [49] and he then begins to beat his fellow servants and to eat and drink with drunkards. [50] The master of that servant will

come on a day when he does not expect him and at an hour he is not aware of. [51] He will cut him to pieces and assign him a place with the hypocrites, where there will be weeping and gnashing of teeth. (Matt 24:4-51)

APPENDIX 3:
BOOKS ON CHRISTIAN APOLOGETICS

Evidence for the truth of the Bible:

There are dozens of excellent books on the topic of Christian apologetics. A few of my favorite follow:

Ankerberg, John & Weldon, John, *Ready With An Answer*, Harvest House, Eugene, 1997, 404 pp.

Craig, William, *Reasonable Faith, Christian Truth and Apologetics*, Crossway Books, Wheaton, 1994, 350 pp.

Lewis, C. S., *Mere Christianity*, MacMillan, N.Y., 1952, 1990 pp.

McDowell, Josh, *A Ready Defense*, Thomas Nelson, Nashville, 1993, 495 pp.

McDowell, Josh, *The New Evidence That Demands A Verdict*, Thomas Nelson, Nashville, 1999, 760 pp.

Strobel, Lee, *The Case for Christ*, Zondervan, Grand Rapids, 1998, 292 pp.

Strobel, Lee, *The Case for Faith*, Zondervan, Grand Rapids, 2000, 286 pp.

For those people who doubt even the existence of a Creator, God:

The following books give incontrovertible evidence that the universe, the earth, and mankind required a Creator.

Ankerberg, John & Weldon, John, *Darwin's Leap of Faith*, Harvest House, Eugene, 1998, 392 pp.

Behe, Michael, *Darwin's Black Box*, The Free Press, N.Y., 1996, 307 pp.

Behe, Michael, *The Edge of Evolution*, The Free Press, N.Y., 2007, 320 pp.

Denton, Michael, *Evolution, A Theory In Crisis*, Adler and Adler, Bethesda, 1986, 368 pp.

Ferguson, Kitty, *The Fire In The Equations; Science, Religion, and the Search for God*, Eerdmans Publishing, Grand Rapids, 1994, 308 pp.

Geisler, Norman & Turek, Frank, *I Don't Have Enough Faith to be an Atheist*, Crossway Books, Wheaton, 2004, 448 pp.

Heeren, Fred, *Show Me God*, Day Star Publications, Wheeling, 2000, 407 pp.

Johnson, Philip, *Darwin on Trial*, Intervarsity Press, Downers Grove, 1993, 220 pp.

Moreland, J.P., Editor, *The Creation Hypothesis, Scientific Evidence for an Intelligent Designer*, Intervarsity Press, Downers Grove, 1994, 331 pp.

Pun, Pattle, *Evolution, Nature And Scripture In Conflict?* Zondervan, Grand Rapids, 1982, 336 pp.

Ross, Hugh, *The Creator and the Cosmos*, NavPress, Colorado Springs, 2001, 266 pp.

Ross, Hugh, *The Fingerprint of God*, Promise Publishing, Orange, 1991, 233 pp.

Wells, Jonathan, *Icons of Evolution*, Regnery Press, Washington, 2000, 338 pp.

END NOTES

Section 1 – God Will Restore Israel in the End Times

1. Hitchcock, Mark, *The Amazing Claims of Bible Prophecy*, Harvest House Publishers, Eugene, 2010, p. 97.
2. Bensadoun, Daniel, "This Week in History - Revival of the Hebrew Language," Jerusalem Post, October 15, 2010, www.jpost.com/JewishWorld/JewishNews/Article.aspx?id=191505.
3. "Against All Odds," American Trademark Pictures, Chicago, 2007.
4. Raved, Ahiya, "Vatican Also Wants Jerusalem?" January 4, 2006, www.ynetnews.com/articles/0,7340,L-3194646,00.html.
5. David, George, *Fulfilled Prophecies that Prove the Bible*, Philadelphia, The Million Testaments Campaign, 1931, p. 90.
6. McDowell, Josh, *Evidence that Demands a Verdict*, Here's Life Publishers, Inc., San Bernardino, 1979, p. 311.
7. Ibid, 312.
8. Stoner, Peter, *Science Speaks: An Evaluation of Certain Christian Evidences*, Moody Press, Chicago, 1963.
9. "Forest and Ecology," www.jnf.org/work-we-do/our-projects/forestry-ecology.

10. Jeffrey, Grant, *Armageddon, Appointment with Destiny*, Frontier Research Publications, Inc., Toronto, 1997, p.273.

11. Mark Twain, *Innocents Abroad*, London: Chatto and Windus, 1881.

12. Fedler, John, "Israeli Agriculture: Coping With Growth," Jewish Virtual Library, www.jewishvituallibrary.org/jsource/agriculture/aggrowth.html.

13. "Agriculture in Israel," Wikipedia, http://en.wikipedia.org/wiki/Agriculture_in_Israel.

14. "Israeli Wine," www.bernardswinegallery.com/pdf/Israel/Israel.pdf.

15. Rosenberg, Joel, *Epicenter*, Tyndale House, Carol Stream, 2006, p. 58-61.

16. Stahl, Julie, CBN News Mideast Correspondent, "Jackpot; Israel on Cusp of Energy Revolution," July 11, 2011, http://www.oilinisrael.net/top-stories/jackpot-israel-on-cusp-of-energy-revolution

17. "What a Gas!" http://www.economist.com/node/17468208

18. Fink, Jim, "Israel's Huge Natural Gas Discovery," Jan. 21, 2011, http://www.investingdaily.com/11168/israels-huge-natural-gas-discovery

19. Levinson, Charles & Chazan, Guy, "Big Gas Find Sparks a Frenzy in Israel," Wall Street Journal, December 30, 2010, http://online.wsj.com/article/SB10001424052970204204004576049842786766586.html

20. Fink, Jim.

21. "Israel Oil Sharpens Med Energy Scrap," http://www.upi.com/Business_News/Energy- Resources/2012/03/15/Israel-oil-find-sharpens-Med-energy-scrap/UPI-41621331840459.

22. Stahl, Julie.

23. Rosenberg, Joel, *Epicenter*, Tyndale House, Carol Stream, 2006, p. 65.

24. Jeffrey, Grant, *The New Temple and the Second Coming*, Waterbrook Press, Colorado Springs, 2009, p. 96-99.

25. "Blueprints for the Holy Temple," The Temple Institute, www.templeinstitute.org/blueprints-for-the-holy-temple. htm.

26. Jeffrey, *The New Temple and the Second Coming*, 55-58.

27. Jeffrey, *The New Temple and the Second Coming*, 55-58.

28. Jeffrey, Grant, *Armageddon, Appointment with Destiny*, Frontier Research Publications, Inc., 1997, p. 141-145.

29. Jeffay, Nathan, "Dyeing To Be Holy," 10/13/2010, http:// forward.com/articles/132096/dyeing-to-be-holy.

30. Ibid.

31. Johnson, Lanny and Marilyn, "The Crimson or Scarlet Worm," www.discovercreation.org/newsletters/TheCrimson OrScarletWorm.htm.

32. Temple Talk, "A Red Heifer is Alive and Well in Israel – part 2," www.israelnationalnews.com/Radio/Player. aspx#0#2001#2 (show played on 3/2/2010)

33. Stoll, Ira, "Iraq's WMD Secreted in Syria, Sada Says," http:// www.nysun.com/foreign/iraqs-wmd-secreted-in-syria-sada-says/26514.

34. "FBI Chief: Muslim Brotherhood Supports Terrorism," Feb. 10, 2011, www.investigativeproject.org/2581/fbi-chief-muslim-brotherhood-supports-terrorism.

35. "Ibrahim: Muslim Brotherhood Declares 'Mastership of World' as Ultimate Goal," http://www.jihadwatch. org/2012/01/ibrahim-muslim-brotherhood-declares-ultimate-goal-mastership-of-world.html.

36. "Stand With Us," www.standwithus.com/app/inews/view_n. asp?ID=1757.

37. "Muslim Brotherhood: Israel Peace Deal Isn't Binding," Roi Kais, Jan. 1, 2012, www.ynetnews.com/articles/0,7340,L-4169609,00.html.

38. "Stand With Us."

39. "Qaradawi's Extremism Laid Bare," Feb. 6, 2009, http://www.investigativeproject.org/992/qaradawis-extremism-laid-bare.

40. "Egypt's new president moves into his offices, begins choosing a Cabinet," June 25, 2012, http://www.cnn.com/2012/06/25/world/africa/egypt-politics/index.html.

41. "Muslim Brotherhood Raising Jordan to Boiling Point," Tzvi Ben Gedalyahu, Nov. 29, 2011, http://www.israelnationalnews.com/News/News.aspx/150212.

42. LaHaye, Tim and Hindson, Ed, *The Popular Bible Prophecy Commentary*, Harvest House, Eugene, 2006, p. 191.

43. "The Global Muslim Brotherhood Daily Report," http://globalmbreport.org/?p=5398.

44. Glaser, John, "Russia Warns Against US Attack on Iran," January 19, 2012, http://news.antiwar.com/2012/01/19/russia-warns-against-us-attack-on-iran.

45. Wagner, Janet, "Russia massing troops near northern Iranian border?" April 10, 2012, http://theextinctionprotocol.wordpress.com/2012/04/10/russian-massing-troops-near-nothern-iranian-border.

46. Sakelbeck, Erick, "Mahdi Video Exposure Rattles Iranian Regime," www.cbn.com/cbnnews/world/2011/April/Mahdi-Video-Exposure-Rattles-Iranian-Regime.

47. Jeffrey, Grant, *Armageddon, Appointment With Destiny*, Frontier Research Publications, Toronto, 1997, p. 288.

48. Robertson, Campbell, "Iraq Suffers as the Euphrates River Dwindles," July 13, 2009, http://www.nytimes.com/2009/07/14/world/middleeast/14euphrates.html.

49. Dugger, A. N., "Miracles of the Six Day War," http://freepages.religions.rootsweb.ancestry.com/~jimmylewis/6daywar.html.

50. "Hidden Miracles - the spiritual dimension," www.sixdaywar. co.uk/hidden_miracles.htm.

51. "Gershon Salomon Saved by God's Angels," http:// miraclechrist.blogspot.com/2010/04/gershon-salomom-saved-by-gods-ang.

52. "Against All Odds – discs 1&2," American Trademark Pictures, Chicago, 2007.

53. "Miracles in the Six-Day War: Eyewitness Accounts," www. israelnationalnews/News?News.aspx/122435.

54. Ibid.

55. Ibid.

56. "The Presence of God in the Six Day War," www. thechurchofgod.com/The%20Presence%20of%20God%20 in%20the%.

57. "Against All Odds – discs 1&2," American Trademark Pictures, Chicago, 2007.

Section 2- The World in the Latter Days

1. Jeremiah, David, *What In The World Is Going On?* Thomas Nelson, Nashville, 2008, p. 58.

2. Amadio, Kimberly, "The EU has Replaced the U.S. as the World's Largest Economy," http://useconomy.about.com/od/ grossdomesticproduct/p/largest_economy.htm.

3. "Eisenhower's Farewell Address," http://en.wikisource.org/ wiki/Eisenhower's_farewell_address.

4. The Power Hour, www.thepowerhour.com/news3/jfk_ speech_transcript.htm.

5. Jeffrey, Grant, *Final Warning*, Frontier Research Publications, Inc., Canada, 1995, p. 74.

6. Ibid., 76.

7. "Thirst For Justice," Melvin Sickler, www.prolognet.qc.ca/ clyde/cfr.html.

8. Ibid.
9. Ibid.
10. Saul Mendlovitz, Director World Order Models Project, 1975, www.siliconinvestor.com/subject.aspx?subjectid=54189.
11. Jeffrey, Final Warning, 82.
12. "The 'New World Order,'" http://www.casescorner.com/id18.html.
13. "New World Order: Quotes of Note," www.greaterthings.com/Conspiracy/NewWorldOrder/NWO_quotes.htm.
14. "Revisiting Walter Cronkite and Hiliary Clinton's Call for global governance," http://www.renewamerica.com/article/050524.
15. Ibid.
16. "Henry Kissinger and the New World Order," http://www.youtube.com/watch?v=HfK0tvk7VNk.
17. "The 'New World Order.'"
18. "Who Will the U.S. Bow to Next? http://www.lastgeneration.us/eleven_twentynine_nine.html.
19. Jeffrey, *Final Warning*, 98.
20. Jeffrey, *Final Warning*, 98.
21. Jeffrey, Final Warning, 98.
22. "A Warning Voice to Wake up America," http://awarningvoice.com/crisis.html.
23. "Never Waste a Good Crisis, Clinton Says on Climate," http://in.reuters.com/article/2009/03/06/us-eu-climate-clinton-idINTRE5251VN20090306.
24. Myers, Steven, "A Triage to Save the Ruins of Babylon," www.nytimes.com/2011/01/03/arts/03babylon.html?_r=1.
25. "Mexican Officials and Police Get Microchips," www.youtube.com/watch?r=aayLSRLYdYY.
26. Rosenberg, Joel, *Epicenter*, Tyndale House, Carol Stream, 2006, p. 203-223.
27. Ibid.

28. Mitchell Chris, CBN News Mideast Bureau Chief, "Visions of Jesus Stir Muslim Hearts," www.cbn.com/spirituallife/onlinediscipleship/understandingislam/Visions.aspx.

29. Rosenberg, 219.

30. Mitchell.

31. Mitchell.

32. Segal, Sarah, "Evangelists Say Muslims Coming to Christ at Historic Rate," www.charismamag.com/index.php/news-old/29125-evangelists-say-muslims-coming-.to-christ-at-historic-rate.

33. "The Jesus Visions," www.jesusvisions.org/index.shtml.

34. "Dreams Draw Six Million + Muslims to Jesus," http://whygodreallyexists.com/archives/dreams-draw-6-million-muslims-to-jesus.

35. Rosenberg, 220.

Section 3 – The Olivet Discourse: Jesus Tells of the Signs of His Coming

1. Ruggirello, Tom, "Prosperity Theology," http://www.heraldmag.org/2011/11mj_7.htm.

2. "Oprah Winfrey: Jesus Did Not Come To Die On The Cross," http://www.youtube.com/watch?v=xM5ILOsHLnw&feature=related.

3. "Secular Humanism," http://www.wordthrill.com/define/secular+humanism.

4. "What is Secular Humanism," www.christiananswers.net/q-sum/sum-r002.html.

5. Cloud, David, "The World Council of Churches," Way of Life Literature, www.wayoflife.org/database/wcc.html.

6. Ibid.

7. "20th Century Saw 65% of Christian Martyrs," www.freerepublic.com/focus/news/681473/posts.

8. Ibid.

9. "History of Anti-Semitism, The Southern Institute for Education and Research," http://www.southerninstitute. info/holocaust_education/ds1.html.

10. "One in Three Spaniards is Anti-Semitic," T.O.T. Consulting, September 12, 2010, http://privateinvesigations.blogspot. com/2010/09/poll-one-in-three-spaniards-is-anti.html.

11. Urban, Susan, "Anti-Semitism in Germany Today," http:// www.jcpa.org/phas/phas-urban-f04.htm.

12. "Antisemitic Hate Crimes Rise in 2009," http://www. thelocal.se/27560/20100702.

13. "Why Do the Nations Hate Israel?" Church and Israel Forum, www.churchisraelforum.com/why_do_the_nations_ hate_israel.htm.

14. Gingrich, Newt, July 10, 1997, htttp://c-spanvideo.org/ videoLibrary/clip.php?appid=596881868.

15. "The Boxer Rebellion," http://www.cmalliance.org/about/ history/in-the-line-of-fire/boxer-rebellion.

16. Jeffrey, Grant, *Armageddon, Appointment with Destiny*, Frontier Research Publications, Inc., 1997, p. 261-264.

17. Ibid.

18. "Signs of the End," http://www.countdown.org/posters/ text/signstime.htm.

19. Jeffrey, *Armageddon, Appointment with Destiny*, p. 236.

20. Jeffrey, *Armageddon, Appointment with Destiny* p. 232-240.

21. Jeffrey, *Armageddon, Appointment with Destiny*, p. 235.

22. Jeffrey, *Armageddon, Appointment with Destiny*, p. 235.

23. "Arms Industry," Wikipedia, http://en.wikipedia.org/wiki/ Arms_industry.

24. "One Billion People Hungry," http://www.thenigerianvoice. com/nvnews/36168/1/one-billion-people-hungry.html.

25. "Food Security," Wikipedia, http://en.wikipedia.org/wiki/ Food_security.

26. "One Billion People Hungry."

27. "One Billion People Hungry."

28. "Famine Declared as Drought Ravages Somalia," http://www.abc.net.au/news/2011-07-20/famine-declared-as-drought-ravages-somalia/2803292.

29. Jeffrey, *Armageddon, Appointment with Destiny*, 241-243.

30. "Population Growth Rates," http://geography.about.com/od/populationgeography/a/populationgrow.htm.

31. "AIDS Pandemic," Wikipedia, http://en.wikipedia.org/wiki/AIDS_pandemic.

32. "Global Trends in AIDS Mortality," http://www.popcouncil.org/pdfs/wp/pgy/016.pdf.

33. "Global Spread of H5N1," Wikipedia, http://en.wikipedia.org/wiki/Global_spread_of_H5N1.

34. "Q&A on Malaria Mortality Estimates," World Health Organization, February 12, 2012, http://www.who.int/malaria/world_malaria_report_2011/WHOGMP_burden_estimates_qa.pdf.

35. "Seemingly Insurmountable Hurdles," http://www.watchtower.org/e/200701/article_02.htm.

36. "Avian Flu," http://www.westernbotanicals.com/en/oct051.html.

37. "Why Superfund Was Needed," http://www.epa.gov/aboutepa/history/topics/cercla/04.html.

38. "Global Frequency of Category 9 Earthquakes," http://geology.gsapubs.org/content/36/3/263.abstrac.

39. "Tornadoes of 2011," Wikipedia, http://en.wikipedia.org/wiki/Tornadoes_of_2011.

40. "2011 Tornado Information," National Oceanic and Atmospheric Administration, March 20, 2012, http://www.noaanews.noaa.gov/2011_tornado_information.html.

41. Schneider, Bonnie, "Will 2012 be another crazy year for weather?" www.hlntv.com/article/2012/01/05/extremme-weather-outlook-2012.

42. "2012 Tornado Season off to Explosive Start," http://www.popularmechanics.com/science/environment/natural-disasters/2012-tornado-season-off-to-explosive-start-7136660.

43. "Abortion," Wikipedia, http://en.wikipedia.org/wiki/Abortion.

44. "U.S. Abortion Statistics," www.abort73.com/abortion_facts/us_abortion_statistics.

45. "Reasons U.S. Woman Have Abortions," www.guttmacher.org/pubs/journals/3711005.pdf.

46. "Rape Statistics," Wikipedia, http://en.wikipedia.org/wiki/Rape_statistics.

47. "White Slave Trade Profit From the Crisis," Petar Petrov, 2011, www.presseurop.eu/en/content/article/1070101-white-slave-trade-profits-crisis.

48. "1.2 million Child Prostitutes in India," http://news.change.org/stories/12-million-child-prostitutes-in-india.

About the Author

DAVID SCOTT NICHOLS, M.D., M.S. has been keenly interested in the study of eschatology (end-time prophecy) since his teenage years. He has read and studied on this topic throughout much of the last forty-five years. Although not formally trained in theology, Dr. Nichols spent several years in the 1980s studying the Bible through the Liberty Home Bible Institute. In the last five years, he has reduced his medical practice in order to spend even more time researching, writing, and teaching on a wide variety of biblical topics. For many years, his primary mission activity has been teaching the Bible in retirement and assisted living centers. Since the study of eschatology has always been a most intriguing topic to him, he decided to write this book for publication.

Originally, Dr. Nichols planned a career in the field of engineering. He graduated *magna cum laude*, with general and departmental honors, while receiving a bachelor's degree in engineering science from the University of Miami. While studying biomedical engineering at the highly acclaimed Massachusetts Institute of Technology, he became very interested in the field of medicine. Therefore, after receiving his master's degree, he immediately entered the University of Miami School of Medicine. Four years later, he graduated first in his class.

After spending thirteen years as an officer and physician in the United States Air Force, Dr. Nichols settled into a civilian practice in Brandon, Florida. He has been blessed with a wonderful Christian wife, Sandra, and two beautiful Christian daughters, Laura and Christine. He also has experienced the joy of the birth of his first granddaughter... lovely little Sarah, who just recently turned four years old.

In summary, David is an evangelical Christian who loves the Lord and the study of His Word. He has taken the opportunity that God has given him to study and teach the Bible throughout his lifetime. Dr. Nichols is more convinced than ever that the Second Coming of Jesus is close at hand. This book was written to share the many reasons he has found that led him to that conclusion. It is his prayer that this information will bless Christians and lead many other readers to a saving relationship with the Lord Jesus. This is a book of hope, not of impending doom. God's future for those who love Him will be eternally satisfying and glorious.

Printed in Great Britain
by Amazon.co.uk, Ltd.,
Marston Gate.